you
and **your child**

GW00691639

other titles in the You and Your Child Series
Editor, Dr A. H. Brafman

you and your baby: a baby's emotional life
Frances Thomson Salo

you and your toddler
Jenny Stoker

ORDERS
tel: +44 (0)20 8969 4454; fax: +44 (0)20 8969 5585
email: shop@karnacbooks.com
www.karnacbooks.com

you
and your child

making sense of learning disabilities

Sheila and Martin Hollins

You and Your Child Series
Editor, Dr A. H. Brafman

KARNAC

LONDON　　·　　NEW YORK

First published in 2005 by
H. Karnac (Books) Ltd.
6 Pembroke Buildings, London NW10 6RE

Copyright © 2005 Sheila and Martin Hollins

The rights of Sheila and Martin Hollins to be identified as the authors
of this work have been asserted in accordance with §§ 77 and 78 of the
Copyright Design and Patents Act 1988.

All rights reserved. No part of this publication may be reproduced,
stored in a retrieval system, or transmitted, in any form or by any
means, electronic, mechanical, photocopying, recording, or otherwise,
without the prior written permission of the publisher.

British Library Cataloguing in Publication Data

A C.I.P. for this book is available from the British Library

ISBN: 1-8775-363-1

10 9 8 7 6 5 4 3 2 1

Edited, designed, and produced by Communication Crafts

Printed in Great Britain

www.karnacbooks.com

to our own children
for everything they have taught us

picture credits

The pictures in the book were originally prepared for the Books Beyond Words Series of picture books for non-readers (see Resources).

p. 6: "Family picture", by Beth Webb, from *When Dad Died* by Sheila Hollins & Lester Sireling.

p. 21: "Computer/scan", by Denise Redmond.

p. 27: "A new baby in the family", by Beth Webb.

p. 31: "Parents and pushchairs", by Denise Redmond.

p. 46: "Birthday party", by Beth Webb.

p. 51: "Five in a Ring", by Beth Webb, from *Hug Me, Touch Me* by Sheila Hollins & Terry Roth.

p. 61: "Child in assessment", by Beth Webb.

p. 65: "Parent and child on the way to school", by Beth Webb.

p. 74: "Two girls", by Catherine Brighton, from *Susan's Growing Up* by Sheila Hollins & Valerie Sinason.

p. 83: "On a bus", by Lisa Kopper, from *Getting on with Epilepsy* by Sheila Hollins, Jane Bernal, & Alice Thacker.

p. 94: "Food being thrown", by Beth Webb, from *When Dad Died* by Sheila Hollins & Lester Sireling.

p. 100: Gary Butler. Photograph by Paul Stuart from a *New Kind of Trainer: Developing the Training Role for People with Learning Disabilities* by Sheila Hollins, Katherine Owen, & Gary Butler.

p. 103: "Drinking and dancing", by Beth Webb, from *Hug Me, Touch Me*.

p. 120: "Grieving", by Beth Webb, from *Feeling Blue* by Sheila Hollins & Jenny Curran.

p. 122: "R.I.P." With thanks to the person who drew this picture during a clinical assessment.

p. 125: "People near front door", by Lisa Kopper, from *Speaking Up for Myself* by Sheila Hollins, Jackie Downer, Linette Farquarson, & Oyepeju Raji.

contents

about the authors

Sheila and Martin Hollins have a child with a learning disability who is now an adult.

Martin works in science education and has managed projects to produce educational resources for children, students, and teachers, including books and TV programmes. He has a particular interest in child development and how children learn.

Sheila, who was previously a child psychiatrist, works as a psychiatrist and psychotherapist with adolescents and adults with learning disabilities. She has devised and edited the Books Beyond Words series, which was inspired by both her professional and her personal experience and has won three national awards for improving communication with people with learning disabilities.

acknowledgements

We are very grateful to those parents and siblings who shared their memories and experiences with us. The families whose stories we tell have asked to remain anonymous, and some details have been changed to protect their identities.

series editor's foreword

Dr A. H. BRAFMAN

We are privileged that Sheila and Martin Hollins have written this third volume of our series of books on child development. Discovering that one's child has a disability is a painful trauma for all parents. This can be compounded when professionals fail to understand not only the child's complex feelings, but also the sense of helplessness that the parents struggle with. Martin and Sheila have drawn on their considerable experience with these problems and produced a book that portrays with sensitivity and accuracy the problems that the disabled child/young person and his parents have to face and learn to live with.

There is a central philosophy uniting all the volumes in the You and Your Child Series. Each of the authors featured has published papers and books for the academic and clinical communities; the present volumes, however, are specifically aimed at parents. The intent is not to convince but to inform the reader. Rather than offering solutions, we are describing, explaining, and discussing the problems that parents meet while bringing up their children, from infancy through to adulthood.

We envisage that two groups of parents may choose to read these books: some may wish to find here answers to specific questions or to problems they are facing in their lives, whereas others may read them only to broaden their knowledge of human development. Our intention is that the writing should be phrased in a way that might satisfy both groups. There is an attempt at something of a translation of what children of different ages experience in their lives with parents, family, and the wider world. Our authors have based their texts on their extensive work with children, adolescents, and their parents—not only in the authors' private consulting-rooms, but also in schools, community agencies, and teaching hospitals—and, in most cases, with children of their own.

The authors aim to depict the child's experiential view of his life, helping parents to understand behaviours, thoughts, and feelings that the child may not have been able to verbalize. There is no question of being the child's advocate—no purpose is seen in trying to find who is to blame for the problems under discussion. These are, rather, interested and knowledgeable professionals attempting to get child and parents to understand each other's point of view. In our books, the authors describe in detail the increasing range of each child's developing abilities on the path from infancy to adulthood: it is this knowledge of potential and actual abilities that is fundamental for an understanding of a child's behaviour.

Many, if not most, of the books available on child development adopt the view that a child is the product of the environment in which he is brought up. To some extent, this is obviously true: the child will speak his parents' language and adopt the customs that characterize the culture in which the family live. The commonly heard remark that a particular child "takes after" a parent or other close relation bears out the fact that each growing individual responds and adapts to the milieu in which he lives—and not only in childhood, but throughout his life. Nevertheless, it is still true that not all children brought up in one particular home will show the same characteristics. From a scientific point of view, there are endless discussions on the issue of nature versus nurture. However, from a pragmatic point of view, it is certainly more correct and more useful to consider family problems with children as being the result of an interaction—who started this, and when and how it started, is virtually impossible to establish. Through their words and behaviour, child and parents continually confirm each other's expectations; they keep a vicious circle going, where each of them feels totally justified in their views of themselves and of each other.

It is not rare that the parents present quite different readings of what each of them considers their child's problems to be. Needless to say, the same can be found when considering any single issue in the life of an ordinary family. The baby cries: the mother thinks he is hungry, whereas the father may feel that here is an early warning of a child who will wish to control his parents' lives. The toddler refuses some particular food: the mother resents this early sign of rebellion, whereas the father will claim that the child is actually showing that he can discriminate between pleasant and undesirable flavours. The 5-year-old demands a further hour of television watching: the mother agrees that he should share a programme she happens to enjoy, whereas the father explodes at the pointlessness of trying to instil a sense of discipline in the house. By the time the child has reached puberty or adolescence, these clashes are a matter of daily routine. . . . From a practical point of view, it is important to recognize that there is no question of ascertaining which parent is right or which one is wrong: within their personal frames of reference, they are both right. The problem with such disagreements is that, whatever happens, the child will always be agreeing with one of them and opposing the other.

There is no doubt that each parent forms an individual interpretation of the child's behaviour in line with his or her own upbringing and personality, view of him/herself in the world, and past and present experiences, some of them conscious and most of them unconscious. But—what about the child in question? It is not part of ordinary family life that a child should be asked for *his* explanation of the behaviour that has led to the situation where the parents disagree on its interpretation. Unfortunately, if he is asked, it can happen that he fails to find the words to explain himself, or occasionally he is driven to say what he believes the parent wants to hear, or at other times his words sound too illogical to be believed. The myth has somehow grown that in such circumstances only a professional will have the capacity to fathom out the child's "real" motives and intentions.

It is an obvious fact that each family will have its own style of approaching its child. It is simply unavoidable that each individual child will have his development influenced—not *determined* but *affected*—by the responses his behaviour brings out in his parents. It is, however, quite difficult for parents to appreciate the precise developmental abilities achieved by their child. No child can operate, cope with life, or respond to stimuli beyond his particular abilities at any particular point in time. And this is *the* point addressed in the present series of books. We try to provide portraits of the various stages in the child's cognitive, intellectual, and emotional development and how these unfolding stages affect not only the child's experience of himself, but also how he perceives and relates to the world in which he lives. Our hope is that establishing this context will help the parents who read these books to see their child from a different perspective.

A note on the use of pronouns

In general discussions in this Series, for simplicity of language, masculine pronouns are used to denote the child and feminine pronouns the parent. Unless specified by the context, the word "parent" should be taken to mean mother, father, or other significant caregiver.

you
and **your child**

an introduction
to learning disability

Expectations

If you have chosen to read this book, it may be because you have a child who is developmentally delayed or has been diagnosed as having a learning disability. You may have found out about this at or near the time of your child's birth, or it may have come as a much later realization or following illness or injury. Or you may have a professional interest in children with learning difficulties at all ages and stages.

If you are a parent, you have probably felt somewhat overwhelmed and even confused about what you have been told about your child. Having a child who is different from the child you were expecting is confusing, and at times you may wonder whether you "have what it takes" to cope and to be able to navigate in this new and unknown world.

It may be more difficult for parents of children with learning disabilities to access appropriate help and advice if mental health and behavioural problems appear. Despite the availability to parents of a wide range of books covering child development and parenting, most writers completely omit to mention children with learning disabilities. This omission may arise from a lack of experience with children like ours. So why does this happen, and how can we, as parents, adapt all the different theories they write about for our own use?

One of the main reasons we, as parents of a child with a learning disability, have written this book is to emphasize the importance of the parents' understanding of their own child and to help parents adapt what they know about ordinary child development for their own situations. We know from our personal experience that parental expertise is not always recognized by professionals working in the fields of medicine and education. There are times when it is hard for professionals to admit that they lack the knowledge or experience that will help to solve the problem. Sometimes there is such an emphasis on finding a diagnosis or cure that more everyday experiences are neglected. Parents can at times feel they are blamed for being overprotective of their children; at other times they are expected to show great trust in the abilities of others to help.

All of these uncertainties and confusions add to the anxiety any parent will feel for his or her child. For us, as parents, it may seem even harder, as we try to do the best for our children in a world in which they do not seem to fit. We may become known as difficult because of this, seen as making unreasonable demands. This may be due to our unfamiliarity with the system or to the kind of language used by professionals. As parents, we may see some professionals as difficult, perhaps because they seem uninterested in our family's perspective and have strong opinions and priorities of their own for our child. Our hope is that this book can help with this and can also encourage parents to make reasonable demands, knowing what they know of their own child. We also hope that, like us, you will find that, in addition to the unexpected challenges, there will be many unexpected joys too. What we cannot offer in this book are failsafe recipes or handy practical tips. Each of our children is unique and will give us plenty of unexpected experiences, however much we try to anticipate and prepare for them!

What is a learning disability?

The term "learning disability" is imprecise. It encompasses impairments and difficulties of many degrees and of numerous causes. Some children have lesser intellectual ability, which remains uncomplicated by other factors; others have a more mixed picture, with greater ability or disability in one or more areas. Some children will also have physical or sensory impairments or life-threatening illnesses. Some will carry the visible signs of a particular syndrome in their facial or bodily appearance, while others will show no physical indication of difference and will enjoy excellent health. The description of learning disability used in *Valuing People: A New Strategy for Learning Disability in the 21st Century*, the Government White Paper on learning disability (Department of Health, 2001), is included here in full:

> Learning disability includes the presence of
> - a significantly reduced ability to understand new or complex information, to learn new skills (impaired intelligence), with
> - a reduced ability to cope independently (impaired social functioning)
> - which started before adulthood, with lasting effect on development.

This definition includes people with a broad range of ability. Whether someone will be entitled to extra health and social care doesn't just depend on an IQ score of less than 70—the traditional administrative definition of learning disability or mental handicap. Whether they have additional sensory or physical impairments, autism, or impaired communication will also be relevant.

Knowing your changing child

What implication does all this have for parents of a child with a learning disability? You will all want to see your child develop the ability to cope with the world of his future. We think your most important role is to act as an interpreter of how your child is interacting with the world now. This is where the careful, open-minded observation of your child can be so useful. Of course, in a busy day of caring for your child, there may not seem to be much time for "mere" observation. But as parents we need that evidence to make sense of our child's growing understanding of who he is and how he relates to the world. This can be of practical help both in our day-to-day lives with him and to interpret our child to the specialists and teachers.

In this book we are not trying to impose any particular theory—whether educational, developmental, or psychological—but, rather, to stimulate your thinking and encourage you to work things out for yourselves. For this reason, we have not provided many references, although we do list at the end of the book some ideas for further reading and some reliable sources of information. Despite much scientific research, no one knows how to explain all these things. Remember that your child and your relationship with your child are both unique. Since nobody has all the answers, you need to collect your own evidence through observing and trying out your ideas and then modifying them if they don't work.

Each one of us has a working theory of life, coloured by our own personal and professional experiences and our family, cultural, or religious expectations. Such theories sometimes get in the way of what is actually happening in front of our own eyes, causing us to fail to engage with our child as he really is.

How different?

In writing this book for the family carers of such a wide range of children, we have set ourselves a problem. If our children are all so different from each other, what could we say that is helpful for all? Part of our answer is to emphasize that there are many things that we share and many ways in which our children have common experiences and travel common developmental paths, albeit at different rates. There are two main themes: the development of the individual, and the changes that they will face in the world in which they are living. For both of these themes, we set out what might be considered typical or common experiences, both of child development and of social circumstances, such as school and social activities. We then reflect on the ways in which our children are different and how, therefore, our parental experiences may differ. To try to capture the reality of individual difference, we have used stories about several children who have learning disabilities. These stories help us to illustrate many of the ideas and experiences that we write about in each chapter.

Six children with learning disabilities

We have made particular use of the experiences of six children, each of whom faces rather different challenges. We introduce the children and their families briefly here, but you will read much more about them as we move through the different ages and stages in the chapters that follow. The five parents who have written about their children have asked only that their child's name should be changed. Most other details are as they were told to us, and we are grateful for their excellent memories and for their willingness to share their stories and their children's stories so openly.

It may be that none of their descriptions is quite like your child, but we think that you will find something helpful in their experiences. A brief summary of each child is presented here and is also repeated at the back of the book for reference.

Three of the children were diagnosed as having a learning disability at birth:

— "Kirsty", who is now an adult, and "David", who is still at school, both have Down's syndrome.
— "Carol", who was not expected to survive to adulthood, is a 20-year-old with profound and multiple learning disabilities and with very high support needs.

"Patrick", "Neil", and "Jay", now all young adults, differ in the time of their diagnosis, the degree of their learning disability, and the extent of their behavioural challenges to their carers:

—Patrick is autistic and has a severe learning disability and challenging behaviour.

— Neil has a moderate learning disability, with specific language difficulties.

— Jay also has a moderate learning disability, with a specific medical syndrome.

You may prefer to start reading the next section now and refer back to these details of other children later.

Kirsty

Kirsty is the youngest of five children in a family who live in the suburbs of a large city. Her diagnosis of Down's syndrome was a considerable shock to her parents, who had no previous knowledge of anyone with a learning disability. Her mother, especially, as she learnt more about Kirsty's condition, became very involved with other families who had a disabled child. She found that other families valued her interest and support and that this was of mutual benefit. Kirsty had a heart murmur and had regular checks by a paediatric cardiologist until she was 16 years old. She also had a hearing problem and had grommets fitted when she was 7 years old, but generally she has enjoyed good health throughout her life. Having older brothers and sisters meant she had a ready social circle. She attended the local special school for delicate children and did well until she was a teenager.

During a brief period at a school for children with severe learning disabilities, her academic achievement deteriorated. Her education continued in a special class in the local adult education college, and she still attends a part-time basic skills course in maths. Kirsty is now 25 and is a very able young woman, both academically and artistically.

David

David, who is Carol's younger brother and the third child in his family of four siblings, has Down's syndrome. He had initial health problems (co-anal atresia, a bony blockage in the nasal passage), with difficulty in breathing. He had an emergency operation at the age of 2 weeks and on-going treatment for a year. He also suffered from glue ear and hearing problems and had several sets of grommets and "T" tubes, and hearing aids were tried. He also suffered from a constant runny nose and frequent infections. He attended a mainstream primary school and now goes to a local special school. It is hoped he will go on to a local further education college. He enjoys a full social life, including a special needs drama group, youth club, and sports club. He likes going out to football matches, swimming, watching videos, and eating out in cafes! He is a well-built, healthy 17-year-old, showing improved communication skills and sociability.

Carol

Carol is the second in a family with four children. She was born with severe brain damage caused by cytomegalovirus. She had frequent seizures as a tiny baby, and these have continued throughout her life. Gradually it became apparent that she had serious visual and hearing impairments, and cerebral palsy (spastic quadriplegia). She attended a local special school and remains living at home, with her mother as her main carer. She now has scoliosis and curvature of the spine. Carol is now a profoundly multi-disabled young woman aged 20 years. She is passive and quite unresponsive. She is totally dependent on others for all aspects of her personal care and daily living. She often has difficulty eating and is frequently sick. She receives some limited extra help from paid carers and enjoys a sensory programme of activities such as physiotherapy, aromatherapy, swimming, music, and light therapy. She attends a hospice for respite care.

Patrick

Patrick has an older brother and sister and has enjoyed being in the centre of a close family. He was a beautiful baby, and the reality of his delayed development unfolded gradually. He is now known to be autistic, but this was still a little-understood condition when he was a young child and the detailed diagnosis came much later. He also developed epilepsy in his teenage years. Patrick eventually gained a fairly good use of language (although like many autistic people he took a long time to sort out his use of I/you and mine/your). He failed to cope in three special schools before he was 10 years old, and then he went to live in a special community school with the hope that he would move on to a residential adult college and residential care. He has always needed people around him who really understand his view of the world and his fears. In the absence of understanding, his behaviour can become unmanageable, so he has experienced many crises of environment and support. His mother eventually gave up work entirely to be available sometimes as his full-time carer, sometimes as an advocate, and latterly as his care manager. He now lives in his own home with a team of carers who enable him to continue to enjoy the full life his family gave him as he was growing up.

Neil

Neil was born to parents who already had a 2-year-old daughter. Neil now has two younger sisters as well. He was an easy baby, with no indication of a disability until he was about 18 months old, when a hearing problem was suspected and thought to be contributing to his delayed development. Over the next few years Neil had numerous assessments, by doctors, psychologists, and educators, with no clear diagnosis. He had meanwhile attended playschool and a mainstream nursery but still had no useful speech or comprehension. The choice of primary school was made on the basis of the speech therapy available there. The school included many autistic children, though Neil's needs seemed different from many of his classmates. His parents chose a boarding-school for him when he was 11 years old, after visiting many other schools. Its warm, relaxed approach and the way teachers and speech therapists worked together proved successful. Neil stayed on until 18, developing considerable social competence with language.

After leaving school he chose to attend a residential college, distant from home. This was not successful, so he moved to a group home in London, where he enjoyed a close social network both in his house group and in the wider community. He spent most of his weekdays in craft workshops. After a while he decided he wanted to live more independently. He moved into his own flat, sharing with a friend and with the substantial support they both needed.

Jay

Jay is the only child of Indian parents who had come to England a few years before his birth to continue their studies. He is now 24 years old.

Jay has a rare syndrome, with several aspects to it, including learning disability, congenital heart disease, and epilepsy. He also has to face the stigma of looking different—just as Kirsty and David have to.

Jay was assessed by an educational psychologist before starting school and was offered a place in a special school for children with severe learning disabilities. His parents had heard that it was possible for children like Jay to have extra help in order to support them in a mainstream school. A local church primary school accepted Jay on trial for a term, provided that one of his parents accompanied him for at least part of each day. His father worked part time during this period so that he could take on this role, and Jay remained in mainstream education until it was time to transfer to secondary school. Then it was decided that the comprehensive school would be too intimidating an environment for Jay. When he was 18 years old, he developed epilepsy. The watchful eye needed to help him cope with epileptic seizures was more reliable in a special school. After school he had two years in a residential college and then moved to a staffed group home near his parents, where he currently lives. He attends a day centre for adults with learning disabilities.

What about education?

Each of the chapters that follow has a section about schooling, so it may be useful to think about the ways in which the purpose of education is sometimes understood. In the classical or traditional approach, an expert (a teacher) transmitted the knowledge to the unknowing learner. This approach aimed to remedy the learner's difficulty in understanding the world as it is, and how he or she is to fit into the world. This model is easily extended into special education for those with learning disabilities. The deficiency is greater, so the experts need to be more specialized, both to be able to transmit the knowledge and to determine the limits of the knowledge their pupils need.

Over the last century, education has been influenced by a more developmental approach, which recognizes that children have innate abilities for learning and that these change over time. The role of the expert is to decide when these developmental stages occur and to manage the environment so that children are best supported to use their developing abilities. In the case of special education, experts need to modify the learning environment so that those with particular impairments can still develop their innate abilities.

A third perspective might be called the scientific view. This starts from the fact that we now know a great deal about the influences on individuals of both their genetic inheritance and their environment while they are growing up. We also know that the two are interconnected—for example, some people's genetic make-up may mean that they are more susceptible to physical aspects of the environment such as pollution and that this can cause allergies. What we do not have is any detailed knowledge of the relative importance of these factors, particularly at the level of an individual. This is often described as the nature–nurture problem. The scientific approach to this problem is not to apply some complex theory of factors, but to carefully observe individual behaviour. In this way, we collect evidence that can be used to try to explain what *this* behaviour means for *this* child. It is important not to have preconceptions when collecting our evidence, to avoid influencing what we see. Thus we must be careful not just to see the child in terms of his impairment, learning stage, genes, or social background, but to approach him as an individual with a unique mix of abilities and needs.

The structure of the book

The following five chapters are arranged chronologically. It is not necessary to read the book in this order: you may wish to start with the chapter that is appropriate to the age of your child. We have tried to follow a similar structure in each chapter to help you to find things of interest at a particular time. Chapters start with a section on "typical expectations", which summarizes what parents usually expect to find in a child of that age or at that stage. We recognize, of course, that your child may meet some of these stages at later times. The idea here is that some readers may find it helpful to remind themselves about "normal" development. Sometimes it will be encouraging because your child will be experiencing similar things. Perhaps more importantly, it will help you to locate the stage your child has reached in some aspects of his development—regardless of his actual age. This is followed by a section on aspects of the difficulties we all experience from these typical expectations. The next section is broadly related to education, followed by "engaging with the wider world". We end each chapter with what we hope is the heart of the book— "knowing your changing child". The message in this section is strongly expressed in the words of Carol and David's parents:

"Parents are the ones who know the most about their children. We are very much more aware of their personality and are in a much better position to interpret behaviour and language.

"We know the language they are speaking, the words they know, the context in which they are talking—so we understand what others cannot.

"We understand certain behaviours, because we know that they are maybe copying mannerisms that they have seen in others—or even in Walt Disney characters!

"However, we will often be accused of 'rose-coloured spectacles'. We are often labelled 'over-protective' and as making excuses for our children. But isn't everyone like that about his or her offspring?"

All the families whose stories we are telling made similar points in different ways, so to any professionals reading this book: please listen to parents—we know our children!

Towards the end of the book we have written about mental and emotional health, which are relevant whether you are the parent, brother, or sister of a younger or older child. It may be more difficult for families of children with learning disabilities to access appropriate help and advice if mental health and behavioural problems appear. Finally, in chapter 8, we draw some of our ideas together, with some positive reflections on the experience of parenting a child or young person with a learning disability.

2

babies and toddlers

Typical expectations of babies

A great deal has been learnt about babies in recent years that can be of use to parents in understanding their child and their own role as parents. There are many different ways to think about the physical and mental development of a typical child in the first year of life.

Physical development

Babies are born with inbuilt abilities: reflex (involuntary) actions such as grasping, rooting, and sucking; senses such as vision and hearing; perceptions of the space around them; and a capacity for learning. These abilities reflect the state of development of the newborn brain, in which the lower parts of the brain are the most developed. In the first year of life there is considerable growth in the upper part, the cortex, and in the number of nerve connections or synapses, and different parts of the cortex begin to develop specialized functions such as communication skills.

A baby's motor skills develop quickly after birth. One example is in the control of eye movement, which undergoes almost complete development between birth and 16 weeks. Reaching and grasping is apparent in the newborn baby as an involuntary action, and this declines in the first few months of life, to be replaced by voluntarily controlled actions, many of which are quite skilful by 9 months. Newborn babies have a stepping reflex, but this declines within a few months, with most children beginning to take steps under their own control at around 1 year and walking independently soon after. This is often seen as a great milestone, but its timing seems unrelated to future intellectual or other abilities.

A newborn baby appears quite straightforward physically, with its obvious needs for sleep, food, and clean nappies being entirely the responsibility of its parents. Crying is the prompt— but how do we know what the cry means? Initially, crying is not voluntary, in the sense of trying to communicate, even though it is a response to hunger or pain; however, our parental response is voluntary, so we become responsible for this first communication with our baby. The baby soon develops the ability to make connections between crying and the provision of milk, thus being able to initiate voluntary communication itself.

A baby can see and hear at birth, but not clearly. The sharpness of vision, called acuity, develops during the first year, as does the range of hearing. Colour vision develops after about 8 weeks. Babies have a predisposition to look at faces and to listen to speech sounds, both of which are important for their early learning and as "social" responses to people. The ability to perceive aspects of the surroundings develops very early, with some ability at birth. Within the first months, the baby is able to gain a sense of distance by the movement of objects, to use both eyes, and to recognize pictures. Babies appear to be born with a sense of constant size and shape—for example, psychology experiments suggest that when mother approaches, she is not seen as getting bigger, even though she fills more of the baby's view.

Mental development

The mental development of the typical baby proceeds in an orderly way; some things always precede others, leading psychologists to refer to stages. The timing of these varies between individuals, and there is still some uncertainty about what is normal about the timing for the majority. What is certain is that even babies are actively involved in their own learning. The earliest indication of this is seen in the response of young babies to a stimulus. If the same stimulus, say a sound or the appearance of a ball, is repeated over and over again, they will reduce their attention. If a new stimulus is introduced, the attention level will suddenly rise. Babies choose to be stimulated by novelty.

An important feature of early learning is the ability to associate one thing with another—a change of nappy with increased comfort, for example. This enables parents to make use of positive reinforcement at an early age. When we first hear our baby say something that sounds like "mama", we will compliment him with a smile or a hug to encourage him to repeat and improve it, so helping to shape the baby's speech. This approach will be seen as a common strategy throughout childhood for parents to better manage their children's behaviour. It would be a laborious way for a baby to learn language, however!

Fortunately babies have a much more effective strategy for this—imitation. Using their early interest in faces and speech sounds, they will develop the ability to copy expressions and word sounds over the first eighteen months. This does not mean that the baby could learn to speak intelligibly by this time: the baby's brain development would not allow this. The idea of "preparedness" is helpful to understand this. Babies, we have said, are born with some innate abilities. A smile is initially a reflex action. At 8 to 10 weeks, it is a response to some event that results in pleasure. By 4 to 5 months, the "social" smile emerges for people who are recognized. Having been biologically prepared for smiling, the baby learns at a rapid rate. The biological equipment for language development will take longer to assemble, despite a predisposition to learn.

Emotional development

A baby's emotional development begins in the first few months of life, with responses becoming more immediate and appropriate to the situation. This can be recognized in classic facial expressions, such as pleasure at mastering a task, surprise at the unexpected, and anger at the frustration of an action. Attachment to their caregivers develops in these first months of life, and babies will begin to express distress at separation from mum or dad and also at the presence of strangers, in the second six months of life. Usually any distress quickly passes when they are reunited with their mother, and they are reassured by her presence. In this way, the securely attached child is able to use mother as a secure base from which to go exploring. Some children form insecure or anxious attachments, find it harder to let mother go, and then they may either ignore her or show ambivalence on her return. Research shows that children with learning disabilities also form these attachments, although the typical patterns described here may be delayed.

For a newborn baby, the world can at times be a terrifying place. The warmth and security of the womb has been lost, and he finds himself in an ever-changing, often stressful environment. Hunger pangs, tummy-ache, or other physical sensations can provoke intense fear or anxiety—which explains the ear-piercing cries so familiar to new parents! Since a newborn baby is not yet able to make sense of or control these emotions, he depends on his mother (or primary caregiver) to help him contain and manage them. While he does not yet recognize her as a separate person, she is his source of comfort, security, and consistency, holding him together. His attachment to her is crucial in these first twelve months and provides the foundation of his future emotional development. As their attachment develops over the first year, he becomes more aware of his separateness from her and more able to manage his emotions for himself.

Typical expectations of toddlers

Mental development

The big development in the second to third year of life is that of speech. When the different requirements are analysed, this is quite a complex achievement. The toddler has to identify sounds (phonemes), understand the meanings of words (semantics), and learn the rules for making words, sentences, and conversations (grammar). No wonder toddlers are sometimes seen as difficult. Do we recognize how hard they are working? Babies have a predisposition to learn language, but until about 18 months they will concentrate on imitating individual sounds and on understanding and using a few words. There is then a critical period of brain development resulting in the rapid growth of a child's vocabulary as these first two steps begin to be mastered. As we all know, mastering grammar can take a lifetime!

Adults also have a predisposition to teach infants language. We have special ways of speaking to them, including repetitions, simplified grammar, and exaggerated pitch and intonation, and we focus on objects and events that are familiar. The benefits of these to the new language learner are obvious, but it seems that we speak this way without even thinking about it.

In general the change in the toddler's life can be seen as reflecting mental processes rather than the limited physical processes of a baby. Speech is one way of representing these mental processes. Other advances that toddlers make in their use and understanding of representations are pretend play, the use of gestures, and the enjoyment of toy models and picture books. However, their abilities in this respect are still quite limited. They cannot follow adult logic, their memories are very limited,.and they find it difficult to distinguish the real from fantasy.

Emotional development

Managing the behaviour of toddlers is often seen as a challenge for parents. This difficulty reflects the rapid growth of competence that the young child is experiencing. It is now recognized that although part of the parents' role is to impose rules and standards on an unwilling child, the child himself has a desire to comply with parents' expectations. The child's increased thinking ability enables him to be more independent of parents. Toddlers also become much more interested in others, so they will, for example, begin to socialize with other toddlers at the child-minder's. This reflects the start of their self-awareness and awareness of others. For example the typical child will be able to point to his own nose in a mirror at this age, although for those who are developmentally delayed this ability will happen later.

Because of this awareness of self and others, there is anxiety about pleasing others, especially parents, and the beginning of the self-conscious emotions of pride and shame. How parents respond both with encouragement and by setting limits will be important for the development of the toddler's temperament and personality. A secure toddler will have the confidence to explore the world independently, while knowing he can return to his mother when he needs her. With tireless determination and energy, the toddler now spends his days engrossed in his love affair with the world. He grows more aware of his own place in the world and more interested in his interactions with other people. By the age of about 3 years, a toddler begins to show empathy, pride, and shame and gradually learns to control and express his emotions appropriately. A range of factors will affect parents' responses, including cultural practices, family relationships, including the presence of siblings, and the stress on and support available to parents.

Recognizing difference

Diagnosis

The diagnosis of learning disability can be made before or at birth, or months and even years later, depending on the cause. Universal prenatal screening is being introduced throughout the UK, so that in future all expectant parents will have the chance to know, with a considerable degree of accuracy, whether they are carrying a baby with neural tube defects (spina bifida), Down's syndrome, Fragile X Syndrome, or some other major genetic disorder. The expectation is that, for an increasing number of conditions, prenatal diagnosis will be made in the first three months of pregnancy, thus making early abortion an option for those who choose it. Earlier diagnosis also gives parents more time to do some research to find out what this particular diagnosis is likely to mean in practice, before they make a decision about whether to proceed with the

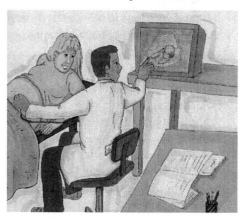

pregnancy. For moral or religious reasons, many will not consider abortion as a possibility, and their enquiries will focus on personal and family preparations to help them cope with this unexpected news so that they can welcome a different child into the world. The Down's Syndrome Association has many requests for information at this time, and they usually respond by introducing the enquirer to another family who have a young child with Down's syndrome.

If not diagnosed before birth, a severe learning disability, especially if it is part of a well-recognized syndrome, or is associated with cerebral palsy, will usually be noticed at or soon after birth. Some babies are instantly recognizable as different in some way.

Jay was born by a Caesarean operation, and we straight away noticed some deformity of his right ear and a skin tag on his right cheek. A few hours later we also learnt about him having a hole in his heart, and we were naturally concerned about his health while at the same time very happy to have become parents. In the following days we were warned that his development may suffer but we would need to wait and see.

For other parents, there is an initial recognition of difference, followed by a period of months during which the extent of the child's impairments becomes apparent.

We could see at birth that Carol had a small head (microcephalus), and over the next few days we were told she was brain damaged due to a cytomegalovirus infection. During the next six months everything went from bad to worse, as it became clear she suffered from spastic quadriplegia (no control over her arms and legs), had severe visual and hearing impairment, and suffered frequent epileptic fits. It was made harder for us to accept this because the medical staff involved seemed reluctant to tell us what they were finding out. There

> was a continual sense of our hopes for Carol being dashed by the next news. I think it would have been better to have the worst diagnosis first, and then we could have appreciated small improvements.
>
> It took about two years to fully understand all the problems she was to have—every day of which I cried in secret.

Each of us has our own story to tell about how well or how badly the learning disability diagnosis was given to us. Much is written about how better to break bad news, but however compassionate the teller, nothing can take away the fact that this news is sad. We parents will often blame the messenger, but the truth is that we didn't want to hear the message. Hopefully we will have been told with our partner, or other family member or friend, and did not have to hear this news on our own. It is still only a minority of medical schools that provide future doctors with much information about learning disability in the curriculum. Those that do, focus more on the medical causes rather than the social and psychological outcomes for an individual with a particular condition. Kirsty's mother describes her experience of a badly informed doctor.

> Kirsty was born two weeks early, and I quickly noticed how different she was to my other babies. She slept a lot and had to be woken up every three hours; feeding was difficult and she didn't put on much weight. When we returned home, I tried to find out about Down's syndrome—the doctor at the hospital had told me that she might not be able to speak clearly, would probably not walk until 4 or 5 years, and her "mental handicap" could mean she would not go to school. The Down's Syndrome Association provided much more positive information, and we met families with young Down's syndrome children through Contact a Family.

Others of us will have faced a slow realization that all is not well, and we may be the ones who have to tell our child's doctor or health visitor that he is not developing in the same way as our other children or the children of our friends.

When he was 18 months old, I wondered if Neil was deaf as he had had several middle-ear infections and seemed rather unresponsive to language. The doctor blamed his slow development on me being a working mother—which didn't help my sense of guilt! This eventually led to a referral to a specialist at a child development centre, who enrolled him in a parent-led home-teaching programme for children with delayed speech and language. Deafness had been ruled out as a cause. We also sought an opinion from a child psychiatrist, and this was the most helpful encounter for us personally. After two visits, the psychiatrist said that he had a severe learning disability and the cause was in many ways immaterial—what was important was that he seemed quite secure emotionally.

Sometimes it is comparisons with our other children that first ring warning bells.

Patrick was different from his older brother and sister. He was an attractive toddler, and family resemblances certainly made him look like their little brother. But he didn't communicate like them. Children get to speak at different stages. But even infants have ways of grabbing your attention and compelling you to have baby conversations with them. Patrick could be in the room with you in his bouncing-chair, and you might be busy with something and then realize that you hadn't "spoken" to each other for thirty minutes. In his cot he would spend many minutes looking at his hands, which he would be rotating in the air over his head. When he got to stand up in the kitchen, he liked to hold on to the washing machine and twirl the knobs for minutes at a time.

Patrick is now an adult, with a recognized diagnosis of autism. The diagnosis took a very long time coming, but not from want of trying to get one. He seemed very affectionate and was never aloof, so autism didn't enter our heads. There were various people who sensed there was a problem early on, one of whom was a friend who was a nurse, another a nursery-school assistant who saw how he behaved in a group. His special-primary-school teacher was puzzled by Patrick's inexplicable distress about certain things but never suspected autism. We were floundering in a sea of difficulties; his behaviour was often impossible to manage, but we had no handle on it. He was so different from our other children. But in brief clinical visits there was little sign of these complex difficulties, and so the professionals could be dismissive in their ignorance of him.

A child's failure to show any warmth and responsiveness to other family members may foreshadow social difficulties in the playground. Such children may have disorders of emotional and empathic understanding and may be diagnosed as being on the autistic spectrum. This is a broad category that has relaxed in recent years from a specific and tightly defined triad of communication, social, and emotional impairments to include a variety of degrees of impairment in these areas. The majority of such children also have learning disabilities.

Sometimes some other medical condition occurs to complicate the extent of a child's disability.

Jay was a happy baby and we loved him very much. When he was 6 months old he suffered from meningitis. This worried us even more because of the possible additional effect on his development. I first suspected delay in his development when I found out in a toy club that he was unable to do the same play activities that other babies of his age could. And then we found that his walking and talking were also delayed, so we started taking him to our local child development clinic. There, first his speech therapist and later his clinical psychologist confirmed that he would make slower progress overall.

A family who already has a disabled child will fear that a subsequent child might also be born with some serious problem. Carol and David's mother describes her feelings when this fear came true for her:

When my third child was born, I immediately recognized that he had Down's syndrome and told the nurse "this baby has Down's syndrome" as if somehow it wasn't my baby.

I remember the doctor saying, "You have to mourn for the child you didn't have." I was in a room at the time, several storeys up, and I could hear some children playing down below —I looked out of the window and saw a lovely little girl. I thought, yes, that was the child I wanted—a "normal" little girl!

I already had a daughter with multiple disabilities. After the initial shock, I decided that I just had to accept him completely and decided to treat him like any other child and not focus on his disabilities, because I could not emotionally go through the upset I felt in coming to terms with my daughter all over again.

Breaking the news to others

If diagnosis is about being told, another aspect of "telling" is how we explain our child's difference to family and friends. What we say will be coloured by our own reactions to the news.

We didn't tell our younger children (aged 8, 10, and 12 years) about Kirsty's condition for about a week, although we did tell our 14-year-old son, other family members, and some of our friends. Some of the reactions were very positive and helpful, some were puzzled and we spent time reassuring them! Our own reactions as parents were not very positive, and we spent a lot of time worrying about the effect Kirsty would have on our other children and what would happen when we got older. We had never seen a baby or child with Down's syndrome before, only adults who lived in a "home" and wore ill-fitting clothes. It didn't occur to me straight away that I could dress

Kirsty in pretty things, that she didn't have to look dowdy like the people in the "home".

Perhaps the most tragic "telling" is when a previously well child has a serious accident—for example, acquires a head injury—that leaves them permanently disabled.

Siblings' reaction

Carol's parents faced a complex situation when their third child was born with Down's syndrome. What should they tell their son, who already had a disabled sister?

We found it very difficult to tell our oldest son about David, who was born with Down's syndrome. He had so looked forward to having a brother or sister "to play with"!

All the way to hospital to meet his new brother for the first time, he asked, "Will this baby be able to see? Will this baby be able to hear? Will this baby be able to walk? Will this baby be able to talk?" "Yes." His dad tried to assure him he would be fine, but a little different, and we mentioned the name of a child we knew with learning difficulties. He related really well with him and got a tremendous joy out of playing with him, someone who was able to respond to him—unlike Carol.

> Later, he heard us talking about having two disabled children, and he asked, "Why did you say that? We only have one." We waited several years to explain to him that his brother had Down's syndrome, because we wanted him to bond with him. It was heart-breaking!

However, our other children do need to know the truth, and it is important they find out at home and not in the playground.

Parents' feelings

One reason for dwelling on these aspects of diagnosis is to remind readers how important our parental responses to our child's difference will be, both for our developing relationship and for our ability to understand and empathize with our child. A mother who is depressed will find it much harder to be in tune with her infant's needs. A baby who is unresponsive or who sleeps most of the time will not stimulate us to respond to him as a more active baby would. This can increase the baby's disadvantage because he will have fewer interactions with people. A father who, rather than sharing more of the caring burden at home, escapes into his work will not be in tune with his wife's growing realization of their child's abilities and impairments. Attending to our own emotional needs is thus vital if our child is to have the best possible start in life. Throughout the book we therefore return again and again to those issues, which influence child–parent understanding and communication.

In our "civilized" society, intelligence is valued and stupidity scorned. We grow up with comments such as "Don't be stupid! What a fool! He's an idiot!" in common parlance. We distance ourselves from such states and project such inadequacies into other people, who are thus marginalized and not part of our social circle. To have a child who might be considered "stupid" requires that we take back our own assumptions and face our fears about the ways in which we ourselves might be considered, to some extent, "stupid". We may be worried about whether our child will be accepted and how we will feel if he is not.

Jay's mother describes her first experience of this:

> When Jay was 2½ years old, I went back to work. The first day-nursery we took him to told us after a couple of days that they could not have him as he required more than usual attention; luckily the second one accepted him, which helped reduce our feeling of rejection.

For a child who does not look different but whose difference is expressed behaviourally, it may be possible to pass as "normal". This of itself can cause problems—for example, if toddler tantrums continue until school age and parents have to explain to shocked onlookers that this fine-looking child is actually learning disabled. This chapter is about babies and toddlers, but what happens if my child remains an infant or toddler in developmental terms throughout life? Is there any value in describing our children in developmental ages rather than using their actual chronological age? The media sometimes describe someone with learning disabilities as having the mind of a 4-year-old or 7-year-old, but we have not found this a useful device. Apart from anything else, although our child may find it difficult to make the same cognitive advances as other children, particularly at the same age, he will be enjoying many of the same life experiences. Our understanding of the world is in part derived from our experience of it. Thus, geography can be learnt in school and from books, but visiting other countries and learning firsthand how other people live is another way to learn it. This example may be more useful later in our child's life, but the principle can be applied now, by allowing our children to see how other children play and behave. Learning by experience can start very early. Start as you mean to go on, and strive for your child to be included, however hard you personally find it to have to make excuses for what looks like age-inappropriate behaviour.

Engaging with the wider world

Many children will be cared for part time by others, while they are toddlers, or even as babies. This first experience of separation will be stressful for both parents and children.

It is tempting to reject playschool as a possibility. We will by now have gained some hard-won understanding of our child's special needs—but how could others know enough to provide suitable care? We may also feel that we have a particular obligation to look after our child ourselves, which might induce guilt if we were to pass this on to others. But most children will be in the care of others, at school, by the age of 5 years, and all children need to be prepared for this major step. Will a part-time arrangement now help prepare for this? Playgroups and child-minding arrangements cater for children in very small groups, and there should be time for the leader to attend to the individual needs of each child. Our child may be different, but are his needs really more difficult to provide for at this stage? We will have to think about how to explain any particular needs our child has. If time is available, a parent can involve him/herself in running the playgroup, so as always to be available to their child if needed. More commonly, it will be possible to spend time with the playgroup leader, to give an overview of any expected behaviour, and to exchange daily reports of variations in activity and mood.

From the age of about 20 months, Kirsty went to a local day-nursery for two afternoons a week. Eventually this increased to four days a week before she started part time at a mainstream nursery school. As her mother, I spent a lot of time there, at the nursery's request.

If we can be satisfied that our child's particular needs are being met, there are benefits from socializing with others, both with children of the same age as our child and with different adults.

There will, after all, be many ways in which our child is similar to other children.

> Neil started attending a crèche, at my workplace, from the age of 18 months. We noted an increase in his independence and self-confidence when he was back home. He attended a playschool part time when he was 2 years old until he was 4. During his time there, he would be engrossed in his own activities, but he seemed content in the company of others and happy to be left there in the morning. He learnt to use a potty while at playschool, well before he would do this reliably at home.

Knowing your changing child

Earlier in this chapter we began to think about how we might explain our child's difference to people we meet. A good strategy is to be able to talk about ways in which our child is similar to theirs. For example, we could comment on physical similarities such as eye colour or the fact that they are wearing similar clothes or have older sisters of the same age. This can

help other people, by breaking the ice, and save their embarrassment if they are not familiar with ways in which some children are disabled. We have a chance to model for others the best way to be with our child. We can reduce the stigma often associated with our child's condition if we ourselves are positive and confident. For this reason, some parents will find it easiest to join a social group or a babysitting circle with a friend who already knows the disabled child. Openness probably helps because, unless others have previous experience of disability, there may be some awkwardness about being inclusive. It is usually our call to take the initiative, even if it means that we have to develop a thick skin and some assertiveness. Our child will soon sense if we are ashamed or disheartened by our encounters with other people.

Psychotherapists in training often participate in infant observation, which involves them in visiting a newborn baby and mother weekly for a year. Observing the mother and baby gives trainees a chance to note how communication between the mother and baby changes over time and how their relationship develops. The trainees report back to their supervisor what they have observed, and they are encouraged to take note of the emotional content of these parent–child interactions. The extraordinary thing is that a huge amount happens in these interactions, and parents too, not just professionals, can learn much by being observant about their own responses to their child and their child's responses to them.

When the infant is disabled, the contributions of both child and parent to communication are just as important, if not more so. Communication skills learnt at this stage will prove invaluable in the years ahead, especially if our child has profound learning disabilities and continuing high support needs. In other words, if it is important for therapists to understand nonverbal communication, it is equally important for parents to acquire these skills, especially if a child will be nonverbal for longer than usual.

This is a useful point to reflect on in terms of the experience of having a child with a profound intellectual impairment. Profound means "unfathomable"—and this is a rather helpful way to think about how difficult it is to fathom what might be going on in our child's inner world.

3

preschoolers

Typical expectations of 3- to 5-year-olds

Mental development

The period leading up to starting school is one of continuing rapid development. Preschool children don't just learn more skills and knowledge, they learn how to think and act in quite a different way from a 2-year-old. At 5, most children are fluent speakers, in contrast to the two- or three-word utterances of the toddler. Through this increased language they show a developing ability to reason about the way the world works. Three particular skills are developed at this age that help them think about their environment: they learn how to classify or group things (e.g., toys by shape, colour, or size); they can arrange things in a progression (e.g., from oldest to newest); and they can make simple inferences (e.g., if Joe is taller than Sam and Sam is taller than Sarah, then Joe is the tallest of the three). This suggests that by age 5 years, children are able to represent many things mentally, though their explanations of things are often puzzling to adult ears as they still lack many important ideas such as conservation of size or quantity. For example, a preschool child will tell you that when water is poured from a short wide glass into a tall thin one, there is more water in the tall one!

Social development

These thinking abilities enable children of this age to engage in fantasy play and to understand the perspectives of others; from this they develop friendships with peers and also an understanding of the role of parents. Their social development is in response to their experience of a rapidly expanding world outside the family. Within the family, their relationships with brothers and sisters become more important. In order to develop relationships with others, preschoolers are gaining a sense of their own individuality at this time. They begin to think of themselves as having particular dispositions, such as being friendly or kind to people or pets. This is the start of building self-esteem, with the help of positive reinforcement from parents and carers.

An important aspect of this is the sense of being a boy or a girl. This shows itself in sex-stereotyped behaviour such as the choice of toys and ways of acting. Boys' behaviour often displays a very physical nature, whereas girls are usually gentler and more manageable. So while a boy may express his self-esteem by saying "I'm the best!" at some game, a girl is more likely to take pride in pleasing her nursery assistant—"She said I am a good girl". Friendships with nursery classmates are common, almost always of the same sex. This supports preschoolers in developing a sense of self which has a constant nature: that of being a boy or girl.

Emotional development

Preschool children also experience rapid emotional development. Their thinking ability enables them to begin to understand their feelings, to control impulses, to tolerate frustration, and to express their emotions appropriately. They can evaluate their behaviour and feel pride or shame in it. They begin to show empathy and understand the need for rules about how to behave with others.

With all these changes to be absorbed, preschoolers need opportunities for risk-free exploration. This is why play is so important at this age, providing opportunities for working through conflicts and anxiety and trying out imaginative ideas and social situations.

By the age of 5, children are able to exert a degree of self-management that is quite beyond a 2- or 3-year-old. In part this is due to them understanding the expectations others have of them. Take, for example, invitations to a child's fifth birthday party. In order to prepare these, the child needs to discuss with parents who his friends are and to imagine what the party will consist of. He will anticipate with pleasure that this is his very special day of the year. But he will have sufficient awareness of others to know that they must be given a good time too. Of course, in the excitement of the moment, self-interest can predominate (as it can in adult parties!), but generally all concerned understand the purposes of the event. In summary, the preschool child will have developed the thinking, social, and emotional skills that he will need if he is to thrive at school.

Awareness of difference

There will be many children for whom the above expectations are quite inappropriate. As parents, we may already have realized from early on that their developmental path will be rather different. Because we will introduce our children more to their peers at this age, this is when we begin to fully recognize the extent of their differences.

For those parents whose children have no obvious appearance of disability, this may be the time when they can no longer hope that everything will be okay. A little boy or girl who, until now, has been "no trouble", or who could have been just slow to talk or slow to walk, is now reluctantly recognized as different.

There are many reasons we may have delayed this recognition: our first child has no one we can compare them with; a second child may be in the shadow of an adored older sibling; regular visitors such as grandparents may offer false hope or reassurance, recounting stories of relatives who didn't talk, for example, until 4 or 5 because "they didn't need to". This is also a time when we as parents may blame ourselves or feel blamed by others for failing to meet our child's needs, albeit needs that we don't understand. We want answers about what to expect, about what is predetermined and what we can change.

Some causes of learning disability bring a well-recognized pattern of physical and intellectual development, for most children born with that condition. Parents of such children can seek out as much information as they feel they need to inform their expectations and aspirations, but a significant minority of other parents will not know the reason for their child's disability. Parents still seeking the answer to the question "Why?" may request second and third medical opinions. Medical advances may indeed identify a cause.

For those with a diagnosis, there have been some remarkable longitudinal studies of the development of children with well-recognized syndromes. Many parent-established support groups have invited researchers to answer their questions, such as why their children all seem to show similarly unusual behaviours or learning difficulties. This is sometimes called a behavioural phenotype and suggests that genetic or other damage to the developing brain has occurred at a similar stage and in a similar part of the brain, so that it leads to similar social and behavioural characteristics. Parents often feel some responsibility, whether justified or not, for such inherited or environmentally caused impairments. Understanding and sharing these feelings is an important aspect of self-help groups. Failing to understand and recognize these feelings can interfere with our relationship with our child and leave him to carry the burden of our grief for his difference.

Every child is to some extent different from the other children in the playgroup or the babysitting circle. But it is not always helpful to focus exclusively on the differences. What about the ways in which they are similar to their siblings and other family members? For example, they may have a similar temperament to a grandparent, a passion for music like dad, or mum's curly hair. It is important to recognize their own individuality and their own particular gifts, too. This is where we as parents need to be relaxed enough to see "our" child, rather than just those aspects of our child that educators and therapists may be defining as impaired. One of the delights of parenthood is discovering who your own child really is.

Developmental milestones—both those read about and also those heard about from parents of children of a similar age—give useful pointers as to what to expect. But your child is different. It's as if your child is in a foreign country where he or she doesn't speak the language or understand the local customs. You are spending much more time interpreting for them, explaining what is expected of them, excusing them for not understanding, and getting used to them being on the "outside". This is a role you are going to get used to, and you may well seek refuge in groups of families who similarly have different children. It is comforting to mix with such "bilingual" families—families who understand the world of typical child development, but who are also struggling to make sense of this foreign world of childhood disability.

Patrick's parents describe how they tried to make sense of an experience he had when he was about 18 months:

> There was a plastic musical box that had a string to pull to produce the music, with a rabbit's face with large eyes and ears that moved with the music. At some point in Patrick's early development, someone pulled the string as usual, but this time Patrick became very distressed at what he saw. Patrick's brain had got to the stage of trying to make sense of

faces and sounds in the wider world, but the rabbit's face was moving in a strange way that did not fit at all. He became frightened, much as we adults would if a creature from *Doctor Who* really did ring the front-door bell. The terror became indelibly linked to the sound of the musical box and was then transferred to all musical boxes, and then to push-chairs which often have them attached, and then to rooms that are clearly occupied by infants and toddlers, and then to ice-cream vans (an example of the consequences of this is given in chapter 6).

Another worry that parents encounter at this stage is the comparison of their child with other children of the same age.

Neil was given a book for his fifth birthday, called *Now You Are 5*, by his grandparents who lived in another town. The book was written for a child who has started school and in a language that many 5-year-olds would understand if read to them. It described the experience of a typical 5-year-old, but its language was incomprehensible to Neil. Neil was beginning to understand simple pictures, but listening to a story without any pictures at all was unimaginable.

How could such a misjudgement have occurred? His grandparents had probably asked the shop assistant for something for a 5-year-old. Everything in the toyshop is labelled developmentally for the typical child. It may be too difficult for grandparents to buy a birthday toy for a 1-year-old on their grandchild's fifth birthday! They may fear that such a choice would be misunderstood or taken as a criticism. They may be really struggling to accept their grandchild's disability.

Siblings also need to make sense of their disabled brother or sister's difference and, as their own awareness and understanding increases, to be able to explain it to their friends. Parents need to talk openly about the disabled child, at regular intervals, as their other children's capacity for understanding changes. In the years during which a disabled child is growing up, siblings are developing their own mental and emotional lives. If a "normal" child only has one sibling and that child has a learning disability, the "normal" child's experience will be very different from that of a child in a family with several able siblings. The number of children in a family, birth order, gender, the continuing influence of both parents, and many other factors will all affect sibling experience of family life. Recent research suggests that, after the mother, the eldest sibling is the next-most-important person in the lives of younger children, often being even more important as a role model than the father.

Another consideration is that a younger child may mimic the unwanted behaviour of their older disabled sibling. Role models can sometimes be an unhelpful influence! Sometimes siblings may need help in their own right.

Engaging with the wider world

Now is the time for us as parents to begin to think much more about our child in relation to the outside world. Mothers of disabled children may be fearful of allowing their children out of sight, feeling that no one else will be in tune with their child's distress signals. This is a dangerous path to tread. A mother who assumes so much responsibility may find herself left alone with it! She needs to learn to share responsibility for her child at an early stage, and fathers have an important role here. In giving mum a break, dad offers a safe alternative encounter that can end in a reunion between mother and child. Sometimes other adults fulfil this role—perhaps a grandparent or older sibling, an au pair, nanny, or babysitter. Such adventures are key to each child's social and emotional development. This becomes more important as opportunities to meet other children, and to join playgroups and nursery schools, become available. On the other hand, being criticized as over-protective is unhelpful, because your child does have additional needs and alternative carers must take note of them and inspire you with the confidence that they will know how to keep your child safe. This type of criticism can come even from close family members or friends.

Answering questions and explaining your child's needs to others is quite a challenge. When a disability is not too serious, a medical "label" can be quite welcome. Parents may feel relieved to have an explanation that removes doubts, and if the cause is medical, then it removes any possible blame from them. Many parents will seek specialist medical opinions, and some will shop around hoping to find a cure—or at least an expert with a plan—that offers some hope for the future. So children may be assessed more than once, by different kinds of experts including paediatricians, psychiatrists, psychologists, and various therapists. Sometimes the results of assessments provide reports or labels but do not lead to any action—what one might be tempted to call "so-what" reports. "So what is going to happen now" asked one mum and dad after yet another report described what their daughter couldn't do. Sadly, "so-what" reports may lead to exclusion from the range of positive choices that are open to other children. We think this is often because although the reports accurately list what is wrong, they fail to note all the things that are right! Patrick's parents stressed how difficult but how important it is to trust your instincts as a parent.

You have to be brave when faced with some kinds of people—for example, some relatives who reckon "that somebody needs to start controlling that child", or a child psychologist at a specialist clinic who twice declared Patrick "to be within the normal range", or an educational psychologist who ignored our experience and denied what we knew Patrick was capable of.

We are our child's strongest advocates, and we need to recognize and describe all his "can do's", likes, and wishes and tell people about them. "When Jo looks at you and smiles like that, it means she remembers you from last time you visited."

Approaching schooling

Children may have been regularly in the care of others and with other children before this age, but now there is the expectation that they will begin to participate in that important enterprise of schooling—in which every child will develop as an individual, but in large and smaller groups of others. Socialization is just as important a function of schooling in the early years as personal education. This is one of the reasons why recently the government has greatly expanded the provision of early education. The "Sure Start" programme has made available free, part-time places for all 3- and 4-year-olds in England, for the first time in 2004. The reason for this has been economic, to some extent, as it will allow all parents to gain employment, if they wish. But it is also seen as a way of addressing the social disadvantage of some children, including those with disabilities.

For parents of a "different" child, this can be a difficult step, because we as parents rarely know how different our child is—much as we might hope to. This can be a problem if the "system" seems to offer a limited range of preschool options, none of which seems quite right. It is worth recognizing that to some extent the parents of all children worry about how any institution could be sensitive to all the needs of their unique child. No institution can be designed perfectly for every individual. But we can expect our schools and nurseries to recognize and respond to the needs of every child in their care.

The organization of special education, the types of schools available, and the assessment procedures vary across the different countries in the United Kingdom and, to a lesser extent, in regions within countries. The arrangements in England are described in some detail in chapter 4.

For most children with learning disabilities, the process will begin with some assessment of educational/social need. A community paediatrician, who will have been seeing the child following earlier concerns by a health visitor or GP, will usually trigger referral for such an assessment. The assessment report should identify any specific provision that is required of the educational system. For example, for a child with deafness or problems of language development, the need for regular speech therapy may be identified or, for a child with cerebral palsy, the need for physiotherapy. Such specific requirements are helpful for parents—it is easier then to find out about the quality and extent of such provision and to satisfy yourself that it is suitable for your child's future well-being.

Problems may arise where the diagnosis of need is less specific. Children may be described, rather euphemistically, as "developmentally delayed" or as a slow learner. Such terms can provoke more questions than answers—so, for example, if she is a slow learner, when will she catch up? Catching up academically is unlikely, but the true extent and long-term significance of any delay can seldom be predicted accurately at a young age. An educational setting may be recommended that seems to offer no clear objectives for your child's progress. This may be presented to you as providing, first and foremost, a caring and supportive environment. How will you know if this is likely to be successful enough?

Statements of special educational need, and reports of assessments, cannot include the fullness of a parent's knowledge. But in making the important choice of an educational setting for your child, you will need to engage with the providers in some detail, to satisfy yourself it is likely to be effective. Do not assume that the professionals always know more than you!

Knowing your changing child

Communication and relationships

Parents are acute observers of tiny changes in behaviour in their babies, and they recognize tiredness, hunger, boredom, discomfort, playfulness, and developing skill. Parents with very disabled children who do not acquire enough vocabulary to explain their own feelings and needs have to continue to depend heavily on such careful, detailed observations. Children with special needs often understand more when they are talked to on a one-to-one basis. David's mother explains:

> David cannot always understand instructions/information given in a large group, because he cannot pick up all the words and meaning. The use of words is so important. Someone asked him "are you afraid?"—but the word David uses is "frightened", so he failed to understand.

Such a lack of vocabulary in a child may obscure his emotional intelligence—particularly the awareness that he may have of the emotional state of those around him. Children who cannot express themselves in words may still have a better understanding of relationships than we realize. A child to whom all words are gobbledegook may be highly sensitive to changes in emotional tone, as well as to nonverbal communication. Parents may try to hide their own distress from their children and belatedly discover that such well-meaning deception causes extra anxiety for their aware, albeit confused and inarticulate child. Family secrets often misfire in this way, when the child's fears about what is unknown may be much worse than the actual secret that parents are striving to keep.

It is recognized that the majority of all our communication, especially where feelings are concerned, is nonverbal. We know that in normal development the first sign appears earlier than the first word, and some children can understand and use many signs before acquiring any spoken words.

How will our children, with their communication difficulties, celebrate their birthdays? As described in the beginning of this chapter, birthday events are designed to match the developmental stage of the ordinary child. Let's consider more about Neil's fifth birthday.

Neil struggles to comprehend the concept of a "friend" and to understand that he will be the reason for other children coming to visit. He has no concept of time, so he lives in a stew of anticipation for days beforehand, in the uncertainty of when the event will occur. His lack of language means he has only a hazy idea of what will happen at the party, built around concepts such as "big tea party", "cake", "balloons", and "games". He certainly picks up the idea that this is his special day, but this just adds to his disorientation. We tried to prepare for all this before his fifth birthday, spending time describing the event, using a pictorial approach—which has often worked well—and by being very responsive to his mood. Nevertheless, the party teetered on the brink of disaster when, after

an hour of ever-increasing excitement, Neil was violently sick among his guests. We quietly removed Neil to bed, where he recovered sufficiently to bid his guests goodbye, thus retrieving the situation. So for Neil there was the chance that he had had an experience that was at least partly positive, to help him next year.

Nurturing talent

As parents, we will be the first to recognize the interests, and maybe nurture the hidden talents, of our children.

Patrick has always loved music. Especially if it is live. Even when he was little he loved to be part of music making—playing duets with Granny at the piano, mimicking a guitarist strumming a tune, or enjoying the band at a local pantomime. Now that he is grown up, many people who meet him comment on how musical he is. They are clearly surprised that someone with learning difficulties should play with such good rhythm on the drums, or be able to sing folk songs so tunefully, or can recognize a concerto by Mozart after three bars.

But Patrick's sense of music may not be different from anyone else's; it is just that he has always listened carefully, hearing sounds that the rest of us often pay little or no attention to. And as parents we made sure he had lots of music to listen to—in the car, at his brother's music lesson, during his sister's piano practice.

This sensitivity to music meant that Patrick could use a happy song or a soothing tune to reassure himself. And when he was upset as a toddler, we could always play some restful tape or CD to capture his attention and bring him back to a calmer state.

At the age of 11 years, we took him to the pub for a meal with the family and realized he was actually listening to the Musak. He concentrated so hard he forgot to eat. By the time he reached the age of 14, he would go and ask the barman where the music was coming from. At his boarding-school, bedtime was accompanied by someone singing a lullaby.

David is not unusual in having a good memory:

David has a fantastic memory for places and people. He never forgets people's names. If we went to a park and had an ice cream from a particular stall, a year later, if returning to the same place, he would remember exactly what he did—and demand an ice cream!

Most of our children's developments will have taken place at home until now and will have been shaped by the environment that we provide as parents. We all need to allow our children space to try out their new mental and physical attributes. Kirsty, for example, was happy in a swimming-pool from a very early age and by 3 years could be described as a swimmer (albeit with arm-band support). We can take the opportunities to watch their play, listen to their expressions, and learn about emerging personalities.

4

children of primary school age

Typical expectations of 5- to 11-year-olds

The pace of change in 5- to 11-year-olds is less rapid than in their early years—thankfully so, most parents would admit. It is nevertheless substantial, though in ways that are usually less obvious. Often there are periods when children just seem to be consolidating advances made earlier.

To take the most obvious feature first: they do change physically, but much more slowly than in the early years. At the end of this period, many will begin another big change, that of puberty, which we will consider in the next chapter.

There are significant changes in children's thinking abilities at this stage, and this is well illustrated in the way the school curriculum changes from Years 1 to 6. In infant school, there is much support given to the child's emotional and social development and to developing communication skills with language and numeracy. Classroom activities consist of straightforward, concrete tasks such as counting and spelling. The wider world is explored through activities that engage the senses directly and may look more like play than instruction.

Mental development

From about the age of 7 years, children begin to be able to reason more systematically, using more than one piece of information at a time. Before this stage, children group objects by single characteristics such as either "red" or "toy people". Now they begin to understand complex classifications, such as that there can be a group consisting of objects that are both "red" and "toy people". This will lead to thinking about how the world can be organized—for example, that dogs, cats, and mice are different but have similarities, so that they all belong to the group of animals. It will take longer for them to accept that humans are also animals.

By about the middle of this stage, children will normally have mastered concepts of conservation. Unlike the example given in chapter 3, the older child is able to take notice of both the height and width of a water container and conclude that volumes of water do not change with the shape of the container. Such understanding makes possible their learning of important aspects of mathematics and science.

Children now make great strides in their ability to learn. The infant-class emphasis on direct experience will be replaced by activities in which children make use of their improved information-handling capacity and memory. They are able to set aside superficial appearance and discern an underlying reality—for example, that although the kinds of places people have lived in during recorded history vary enormously, they can all provide the requirements of a home. Children develop particular knowledge and expertise. Many junior-age children become enthusiastic collectors—of natural objects, toys, information cards, pop-star memorabilia, for example—through which they can demonstrate their competence.

This awareness of their own knowledge and thinking is one of the most significant developments from the age of 5 to 11 years. Because of its nature, however, it is one that may not be so obvious to the adult world.

Emotional and social development

What the adult world does see of the primary-age child is their growing emotional and social maturity. The beginning of regular school attendance is a great challenge to any child, but one in which most 5-year-olds have sufficient understanding of their own and others' needs to thrive, with appropriate adult support. It is sometimes called the latency period, suggesting that in some way their emotions are less available to them, or less affected by significant life events.

Throughout this period, children develop their sense of themselves and others through their close engagement with their peers and with a range of adults in authority roles. Their sense of self will show as an ability to identify their own traits and pursue their own interests, perhaps in distinction from others. They will use social comparisons more widely to identify themselves in terms of groups they belong to, such as sports teams. Their sense of their own gender becomes more marked,

and their awareness and use of gender stereotypes increases. Children may reject an activity or preference, for example, because it is used to define the opposite sex—"dolls are for girls", "football is for boys".

Relationships with children their own age—peer relationships—are very important at this stage. Through these, children can learn about themselves and others as individuals, but also about the complex rules of interpersonal behaviour and the communication skills required to use these rules. They will learn to conform to the social norms of their peer group and understand how this group relates to other groups, such as teachers. They will form loyal friendships, usually of the same sex, and towards the end of this stage will understand the boundaries for interactions with members of the opposite sex.

During this period, children develop the ability to go beyond the simple experiencing of emotions to understanding what causes their own and others' emotions. They learn appropriate emotional responses, begin to develop self-control, and feel empathy for others. Junior-age children develop a strong sense of fairness in their social relationships, and this is the basis of their moral development.

It may also be a time for learning about membership of a faith community. Neil's mother describes how he made his first communion in his family's church.

Neil had not been able to join in the first-communion classes with the other children his age and younger. The catechist had had no experience of children with learning difficulties. We felt sad that he couldn't be included. The parish priest was very helpful and encouraged us to prepare him in our own way, and to say when he was ready. This wasn't easy, as he still had so little means of communication. One Sunday when he was quite calm and relaxed during the Sunday service, he came up to the altar with me as usual. The priest asked if he had made his first communion yet, and I answered that this was "the big day".

The growing-child's world is one in which school provides important socialization opportunities, but which also gives him evidence of current achievements and a sense of future direction in life. He may belong to other social groups through out-of-school activities and after-school care arrangements. At home, relationships with parents and siblings will continue to be important but will also undergo change. Difficult circumstances such as conflict, separation, illness, or bereavement will have significant impacts on a child's social and intellectual development.

Making the most of being different

Needless to say, this period of development will last much longer for our children, who have varying degrees of difficulty in achieving a psychological sense of self or any real awareness of others' inner thoughts and feelings. Children on the autistic spectrum will find it particularly hard to know what others are thinking and feeling. Recognizing and managing one's own emotions is hard enough, especially if one lacks the language to describe them, let alone acquiring the skill to recognize how other people are feeling.

To a considerable degree, children learn how to manage their feelings and behaviour by observing and copying their peers. This is when the advantages and disadvantages of mainstream schooling compared with special schooling are perhaps most obvious. In a special school, a class group is likely to comprise children with a broadly similar degree of disability, but different chronological ages. Teachers and supporters will use classroom-management techniques to control behaviours they find challenging or disruptive, to enable all of the children to engage in some educational activities. There will always be some antisocial behaviour for them to try to manage, and the most disruptive behaviours are the ones that they will be concerned about the other children copying. To an extent this will be true in a local primary school, where classroom teachers have larger numbers of children, many of whom will have emotional needs or milder learning difficulties. But a skilled primary teacher probably finds it easier to establish and sustain an age-appropriate culture in their year-group classroom than will a special teacher in a mixed-age and mixed-disability group. Children are now learning to work as members of a group, sharing and taking turns with each other. A relative lack of understanding about others' needs by one or more members of the group can impede the development of shared codes of behaviour. If the majority understand the rules, they are more likely to shape a shared ethos, even if one or two resist or simply fail to follow what is expected of them. Gradually, as time goes by, even the least able child will learn through being included. Repeated opportunities to learn mean that the rules are eventually learnt in some form by everyone. All children have to learn to concentrate, even on repetitive tasks, and to sit quietly in the classroom when the teacher expects it. Parents may, however, feel that the expectations being made of our children are too different and too demanding, as David's mother explains:

Often, children with special needs display "inappropriate behaviour". There are times, however, when this seems unfair. For example, you may be summoned to school and told your child has hit someone in the playground. However, when you observe the behaviour of others, you begin to question this. I noticed that boys of a certain age, when so-called "playing", kind of hit or punch each other as a form of friendly greeting. When your child copies this, it is seen as negative.

The behaviour of children with special needs is scrutinized much more closely than the behaviour of other children. Often they have classroom assistants or one-to-one help, and their every action is observed. They cannot get away with daydreaming, looking out of the window, or flicking paint. They will be labelled lazy, uncooperative, and naughty.

Adults often comment that children are unkind to each other, especially to those who do not fit in. While this may be true to some extent, it is often the case that children can be more tolerant than adults of people who are different. For example, they may have elaborate explanations about why someone behaves the way he does. This is also the stage when children develop fierce loyalties towards their peers and when lasting friendships between disabled and non-disabled children may be forged, with the non-disabled or less disabled peer watching out for his more vulnerable classmate.

Some children come home from primary school and tell mum and dad all about their day, and other stories about goings-on at school will be shared between parents at the school gate. For the child attending a special school, such sharing is unusual.

Neil's regular response, on arriving home, to the question "What happened at school today?" was "Bus"! It was many years before we learnt about the inappropriate behavioural-management techniques used in his school—ones that might have led us to remove him if we had been aware of them at the time and would certainly have led to questions being asked. What we did notice was that some days seemed to have been more stressful than others, that sometimes he resisted physical contact and was especially sensitive to being told off. What he began to talk about much later in life was of soap being put in his mouth if he was "naughty".

If this seems dramatic or shocking, then reflect on your own school experience and consider if you were ever bullied or subject to over-strict discipline—did you ever share this with your parents? As parents of more vulnerable children, we need to be particularly alert to behavioural and emotional changes in our child so that we can ask questions about possible causes. Teachers or school health professionals may be able to throw light on such changes. If not, they should be equally as concerned as parents. Sharing information and concerns is vital.

Schooling for most children at this age is in mixed classes, thus providing opportunities to begin to understand one's own gender. Often gender stereotypes are emphasized in special educational settings—perhaps as a way of teaching the differences between male and female. Self-care skills may be delayed. Help provided with using the toilet, or with dressing and undressing, can offer opportunities for talking about gender differences both biologically and in terms of typical clothing worn by boys and girls.

Engaging with family and friends

Children with learning difficulties are likely to begin to compare their progress with their siblings. This can have unfortunate consequences. Anxieties about failure to achieve a goal can affect a child's self-esteem. For example, Neil's speech therapist wrote this about him when he was 10 years old:

> He is aware of and embarrassed by difficulties. He withdraws from the struggle, with detriment to progress if he feels another child is overtaking him who ought not to be (as is now the case with his two young sisters—he is very aware of his place in the family hierarchy), or if the right kind of help is not constantly at hand with his language development. If he is aware of failing, this saps his self-confidence and makes him back down from his efforts and discontinue the good progress he makes when feeling confident.

Of course, this can have an effect on the siblings as well, who may become unwilling to share their achievements at home.

This is an age when friends are usually so important, and yet children with learning disabilities seldom make friends. This does not mean that other children are insignificant, or that they are necessarily easily forgotten. Indeed, many children will remember encounters with other children with some intensity, even many years later. This may have something to do with the relative poverty of later social opportunities, or perhaps just the inability of a child to explain that John or Joan is my special friend.

The practical difficulties are considerable if, as parents, we are to nurture our child's possible friendships. This may be particularly difficult if the friend is someone our child has met at the special school he is bussed to every day. Such a child, whose parents we have probably not met, may live in another and distant neighbourhood.

Social opportunities are not, of course, confined to the classroom, and there are many local clubs and societies that are open to all children regardless of the school they attend. Many of the children attending a local club will go with a school friend or a sibling. So what are the challenges facing a disabled child in joining an activity of their choice? Sometimes the club leaders will refuse admission to a disabled child, suggesting that they do not feel skilled or knowledgeable enough to include such a child, or perhaps they do not have adequate help. Parents can offer to provide an extra pair of hands themselves or can arrange for an older sibling or familiar volunteer to accompany the child. Sometimes parents and siblings will be hurt by the seemingly discriminatory attitudes of club leaders or by other children teasing or bullying the disabled child. Often we will be pleasantly surprised by the open and willing way in which mature leaders invite a child to join, while wisely recognizing that they may have some additional needs and seeking to understand and meet these. Sometimes faith communities will be able to welcome disabled children to join clubs and societies such as the scouts, with the added benefit that the child will meet other members of this community.

Accompanying siblings will also need help to cope with the responsibility they are being asked to take.

Schools and special educational needs

Schools

Education in the four countries of the UK is locally administered. There are over a hundred Local Education Authorities (LEAs) in England.

The age at which children are required to attend school full-time is 5 years in the UK, though in many other countries it is 6. For many parents this is a straightforward step. Their children will attend the local primary, infant, or first school. For some, this may simply be a progression from the nursery and reception classes in the same building. In urban areas there may be a choice of different schools, but all are designed to take the full range of children of normal abilities.

For parents of a child with a disability the situation is more complex. Provision for children with special educational needs may take place in mainstream schools or in special schools. Children may be admitted to mainstream schools into normal classes with additional adult support, or into special units or classes where most of their teaching is in a special group. Special schools are designed for the needs of particular groups of children. For example, there will be small teaching groups, with substantial adult support, for those with profound and multiple learning difficulties. The physical environment will be designed to suit those with sensory and/or motor disabilities. There may be additional facilities such as speech therapy, physiotherapy, or psychotherapy.

Collecting children with similar disabilities together in a special school enables the human and physical resources to be more readily available. There are therefore a range of different types of schools to meet different needs. The list of those types of schools in operation in England in 2004 is shown in the box.

These figures are included to show the range and frequency of the types of schools. They do not show the incidence of different disabilities. For one thing, these schools are generally much smaller than mainstream schools. In total, just over 1% of school-aged children are currently educated in special schools. Most significantly, there are different proportions of pupils with each of these disabilities in special schools compared to mainstream schools. A recent study by the schools inspectorate (the Office for Standards in Education: OFSTED) reported that one in four of the 32,000 pupils identified with autistic spectrum disorders are in mainstream schools compared with five in six of 172,000 pupils with moderate learning difficulties.

There has been a considerable change in the way that special education has been organized during the last three

Special needs classification	Number of schools
Autism	53
Emotional, behavioural, and social difficulties (EBSD)	245
Hearing impairment	23
Hospital schools	37
Moderate learning difficulties (MLD)	254
Physical difficulties	74
Profound and multiple learning difficulties (PMLD)	10
Severe learning difficulties (SLD)	294
Specific learning difficulties	24
Speech and language disorders	33
Visual impairment	17
Other	251

decades. Prior to the Education Act of 1981, children were categorized simply according to their degree of "mental handicap"—whether it was mild, moderate, severe, or profound. Each of these groups had different provision; that for the lower two categories was often hardly educational in its objectives, care being the prime concern. The new arrangements recognized that the causes of children's difficulties were complex, including specific learning difficulties, emotional difficulties, behavioural difficulties, as well as mental and physical disabilities. Provision was now required to meet "special educational needs" (SEN). These are identified by the assessment of the child with social, educational, psychological, and medical reports. This results in a "Statement of Special Educational Needs", which must clearly show what is to be provided, by whom, in what way, and with what purposes.

Assessing special educational needs

Parents have important rights in the process of "statementing" under the current SEN Code of Practice (2002) and the 1996 Education Act. If parents think that their child has a learning difficulty and that this has not been picked up by the school, they should talk to the teacher or head teacher. Each school has a special educational needs coordinator (SENCO), who will probably be involved in any discussion. This may result in the provision of additional support or intervention, such as individual time with a classroom assistant. This is recorded as the child being put on "School Action" or "School Action Plus" levels of support, depending on the extent of the needs. Parents may request additional support, perhaps from outside the school, such as an educational psychologist or specialist teacher, which is possible under School Action Plus. If parents feel that this level of support is inadequate, they may ask the LEA to conduct a "Statutory Assessment" of their child at any

time, which can result in the Statement of Special Educational Needs. About 75,000 children in England have such statements.

The LEA must comply with such a request, unless they have carried one out within the previous six months or they decide that one is not necessary; if the latter, parents can appeal to the SEN Tribunal. The statement must be detailed, including consideration of the setting in which provision will be made and the amount of special support—for example, hours of therapy. It is recognized that flexibility may be needed in some circumstances, but the LEA is not allowed to avoid such a specific commitment. Parents are able to express a preference for a particular school, which the LEA normally has to name in the statement. This can be an independent school, so long as it is approved for SEN. A school named in the statement has a duty to admit the child. Being full is not necessarily a reason for refusing admission, but the LEA is allowed to consider whether this is an efficient use of resources if extra staff would be required.

Clearly there is the possibility for disagreement in this. If parents are not satisfied with the proposals in the statement, they can appeal to the SEN Tribunal or to the LEA Parent Partnership. The LEA can amend the statement at any time but should secure the agreement of the school and the parents. Recent experience of disputes has shown that most can be resolved satisfactorily, provided that there is a willingness to explore ways of solving the problems. The LEA Parent Partnerships have begun to develop their roles in this. Some are devising parent education programmes.

Each child with SEN provision has an annual review to see whether provision suits his or her changing needs. This is arranged by the head teacher and should take advice from "all appropriate parties". The head reports with recommendations to the LEA and circulates this to all concerned. If there is a change, parents must be informed and have the right to make representations that may result in modifications. Again, the appeals procedure can be invoked if parents are dissatisfied. Parents can ask for a change in the statement if there are changes of circumstances, but only after twelve months since the statement was agreed.

Including all children

The trend in special education has been to recognize the diversity of needs of all children and therefore to make provision for children with learning difficulties less separate. This approach will continue with new legislation under the Children Act (2004). The *Every Child Matters: Change for Children* programme stresses the importance of all agencies working together for the benefit of individual children. Local Children's Trusts will be set up in 2006 to coordinate the resources of education, social services, and health. The principal purpose is the protection of all children, particularly the most vulnerable. This coordinated approach will have potentially significant benefits for our children, whose care often depends on a range of service providers.

In 2004 the government developed their strategy for special education in the paper *Removing Barriers to Achievement*, which has four key aspects:

- Early intervention, ensuring help is available as soon as possible and that parents have access to suitable childcare
- Removal of barriers to learning, with improvements in mainstream and special schools and better working together to offer inclusion for all children in their local community
- Raising expectations and achievement of children with SEN
- Delivering improvements in partnerships, which includes working with parents.

The strategy paper concludes with the commitment that "we will know that our strategy has been successful when we have ceased to rely so much on separate structures and processes for children with SEN, because their needs are embedded in all aspects of policy and their needs are met effectively in local schools and early years settings".

However, sometimes the changes brought about by inclusion policies such as a National Curriculum for all at similar ages can seem to be counterproductive to parents.

Carol attended a local school for children with severe learning difficulties. There was a wide range of handicaps, and so classes were organized not by age, but by the type of handicap. The school then reorganized into age-related groups. This meant that Carol was in a class where other children demanded much more attention. Though she has great needs, she is very passive and so got neglected in this arrangement. Having to follow the subjects of the National Curriculum made things worse. I remember being told in Technology that she was learning the difference between sharp and blunt, and thinking the only way she could possibly learn this would be if she herself was to be cut! In the later years of her schooling, I really thought the emphasis had changed away from what Carol needed to how she could fit into the system.

The probable outcome of this new policy is that the move away from educating those with SEN in separate special schools to their inclusion in mainstream schools will continue. This has the advantage of keeping disabled children in contact with their local community. The risks are that the resources are inadequate and that the environment may be too challenging for a vulnerable child. Many LEAs are currently developing new arrangements such as linked schools or units on the same site (a community of schools), to offer some measure of social inclusion, alongside some more protected and specialized provision.

As parents we may have to choose between a separate education with children who have similar difficulties, and one in which all children are included, or a combination of the two. In practice the choice will be determined by the provision in your local area, by the assessment of the needs of your child, and to some extent by your preference as parents.

Jay's parents were concerned about whether accepting a special school place for him at age 5 would affect which doors would open or close for him in the years ahead. They thought that it would probably be easier for him to move from mainstream ordinary provision into special education than the other way round.

We were feeling somewhat depressed about Jay's education and future. Then we learnt about an organization for integrated education for learning disabled children and joined it. Around that time an important report was published called the Fish Report, which provided a lot of enthusiasm to parents in our position. We went to meetings and conferences and

learnt about the new "statementing process". We began that rather long process before Jay was to start primary school and found a mainstream school that was willing to take Jay, on the proviso that one-to-one support in the classroom was available.

When the school year started, the authorities were still considering our application for one-to-one support. I took a break in employment to go in the classroom with Jay. It was supposed to be for just a few weeks but turned out to be about a year.

Eventually our application was successful and Jay had one-to-one classroom support throughout his primary education in two different schools. His speech started improving straight away, and we think he benefited a lot by daily contact with his more able peer group. At times there were conflicts between his school and us, but they could be resolved by mutual goodwill and accommodation. We also think that there was a downside in Jay becoming a focus of attention in his class and feeling under pressure most of the time. This has left a mark on his personality.

You will want to discuss the recommendations of the LEA for your child and challenge a particular placement if you think an alternative would be better. This proved necessary for Neil's parents:

Neil was clearly a puzzle to the educational psychologist, even after a long period of assessment. The psychologist recommended a school that offered a general curriculum for slow learners but would not provide for his specific needs. Eventually another school was found. This catered for a wide range of different needs, and crucially speech therapy was available on a regular basis to meet his specific language-development needs.

David and Carol's mother considered her two other children to be reasonably well adjusted to having a disabled brother and sister:

Our youngest daughter was a happy, confident, outgoing child. She loved David and played with him and related to him well, all during her primary years. She always liked to attend his special events and seemed really proud of him. I was told that when they met each other in the corridor at school, they hugged each other. She didn't seem to mind at all, and all her friends seemed to accept him.

However, when she went to secondary school and met new friends and wanted to be more independent and "cool", she became embarrassed and unable to tell her friends about her siblings. When she invited her friends to her twelfth birthday party, she wanted Carol and David to be hidden away! I remember that. We were quite surprised!

Then an incident occurred at school. A boy was making fun of some adults with learning difficulties. It had happened before, but on this occasion it caused her to break down in tears. She told her friends and the teacher that she had a brother and sister with special needs and it was not fair to be so cruel. The school dealt with the incident very well, talking to her and confronting the boy about his attitude. She was much happier after that, because all her friends now knew about her brother and sister, and they still wanted to be friends with her.

In reality, much of the effort involved in introducing our children to the wider world will be down to family members, and one problem we will face is the way in which our other children grow out of more juvenile pursuits whereas our disabled child does not. Patrick's mother explains this well:

I remembered the family therapist who explained about family life cycles, and how difficult it is when your child's disability keeps you back in younger mode when the other children— and you yourself—need to move on. That has produced such conflict of interests, so I dreaded having all three of my children home at once, knowing I simply couldn't be a mother to two teenagers and infantile Patrick simultaneously. I don't feel guilty any longer about not being able to cope with it but recognize it as yet another tough aspect of Patrick's disability and, of course, rejoice that much more on the occasions when suddenly the sun does shine on family life all together.

Knowing your changing child

Neil's parents learnt something else when they were preparing him for this particular holiday:

Neil seemed to know something exciting was being planned. His volunteer link person had come to meet him. We were packing some of his clothes in a suitcase. No one else was packing to go away. It must have been very confusing for him. We drew a cartoon story for him of stick people, representing Neil, his family, and the new people he was going to meet. The cartoon showed him waving goodbye to us and going in a coach with lots of other people. It showed a big building and a bed where the stick person called Neil was depicted lying down. It showed some of the activities he would do such as horse riding, climbing a mountain, etc., but perhaps most importantly it showed him coming home and being welcomed by the family. Neil seemed reassured by his pictures and packed them in his case.

Whatever communication method works for you and your child will be the right one, but it may take time to know what does work!

From when Patrick was very little, he loved visiting churches and cathedrals and poring over their pictures in books. If he was visiting someone's house, we would ask them to find him such a book. For him it was much more pleasurable than having to chat to people. Patrick still likes to leaf through books of this kind, but when he was only 5 he would surprise people with his knowledge about all the pictures. Kindly grown-ups would share the book with him, and they would be amazed that he seemed to know the names and shapes of the churches just by looking at the pictures—even in a book he had never seen before. What they didn't know was that he had spent hours looking at similar books, reading the captions, and using his photographic memory to record tiny details about the church architecture. As parents we used to be quite proud of Patrick's quaint talent. Even though it may not seem productive, it is a wonderfully calming occupation for him.

When our child's cognitive abilities are assessed, and reassessed, only to fall short in some way from that found in their siblings, we parents may find ourselves defending a near achievement of a milestone as being of greater import than can really be warranted. We may fail to recognize that the standard we use for our other children requires regular and sustained performance of the skill concerned. Watching, waiting, and celebrating hard-won steps may lead to a small degree of "grade" inflation—and who can blame us!

David's mother explains how long some stages seemed to take:

My son seemed to get stuck in phases that lasted several years. You imagined that they would be stuck with this behaviour forever, and then later on you couldn't remember the last time it happened!

I remember our son kept escaping—crawling out of the garden, following the cat into next door's garden (through thick hedges and rose trees!) while I was out putting washing on the line, taking my eyes off him for a couple of minutes. Later there would be rings on the doorbell, with neighbours returning him home from the street. I felt like a very neglectful mother!

He used to walk to school in his pyjamas and slippers. He used to disappear in shops and could stay hidden for ages—in a rack of clothes or under a bed. One time he disappeared from Mothercare in a shopping centre. One minute he was there, the next gone. I was absolutely panic-stricken and had to call the police. It was the first time I was pleased to give a description of him and say "he has Down's syndrome!" He was found sitting happily in a men's outfitters in the next street.

This running-away phase lasted several years, but now I can't remember the last time. He wouldn't dream of running away now—he would be too afraid and worried to go off on his own.

Another long-drawn-out phase was "toilet training". The whole ritual took time every day: reminding him to go; waiting for him to perform; cleaning him afterwards. This went on for years—probably until he was 14 years old. Then you realize, sometime later, that you no longer know when he goes to the toilet, as he is totally independent.

The same for getting dressed, cleaning teeth, showering—he needed help for years and now, at 17, he manages on his own.

Sometimes, as parents, we may underestimate the importance of an advance our child has made, not really believing the evidence for it.

When Neil was about 8 years old, his teacher wanted him to learn to say the colours red and yellow, and to understand the number two. Every day for a year, his main task each morning was to colour in pages of pre-drawn rows of two concentric circles to look like jam tarts—red in the centre, yellow in the outer circle! This failed to sustain his interest, and he continued to muddle his colours and numbers and to refuse to sit still for long. We made up a game for him at home with his wooden train, trucks, and coloured bricks. We made four train stations out of similar plain boxes and named them red, blue, yellow, and green, the labels being written in the same colour ink as the name of the station. The trucks were loaded with coloured bricks; red bricks were unloaded at the red station, yellow at the yellow station, and so on. Then the station labels were changed for labels written in black ink. After a while, the position of the stations was changed to check that he did understand the different colours, not only as the "concept" colour, but also as the written word for each colour. We were confident that his word-finding difficulty was the problem, not his lack of a colour concept.

This successful home learning was not welcomed by Neil's teacher, however, who declined to participate in his annual review, feeling that we should leave his education to the experts. We wondered if her response was an indication of how unskilled she felt without any qualification in special education.

Such rebuffs are not the norm, but when parents are criticized in this way it can leave them feeling angry and impotent, even when the rebuff was linked to a breakthrough in their own understanding of their child. One key learning point here is that Neil's parents were able to support each other in their encounters with this teacher and this school. A single parent may need to find someone else to accompany her on such occasions. It's a brave person who confronts such situations alone.

Even when we look forward to our child becoming a teenager, we will realize we still have much to learn about him. Some parents begin to lose hope at this stage, as the true realization of the extent of their child's difficulties, and their long-term nature, can no longer be avoided. Taking a break can be a good idea, and hopefully there will be relatives, or respite care arrangements available, to provide excellent substitute care for a couple of weeks, while we and our other children recharge our batteries and try to put things into perspective.

teenagers

Typical expectations of 11- to 16-year-olds

The 11 to 16 age group is socially defined by attendance at secondary school or its equivalent. For the young people themselves, it will be characterized by the physical and emotional changes of puberty and adolescence. As in previous chapters, we present a brief summary of the typical mental and physical development of 11- to 16-year-olds, for reference. As parents of a young disabled person, we will know quite a lot by this stage in their lives, about how different they are from this usual pattern of development. There will probably be delays in both cognitive and emotional aspects of their development, which results in distinctive emotional and behavioural responses and causes personal and social difficulties. We consider these later in the chapter.

Physical changes

This is a period of significant change for any child approaching adulthood. At puberty there are important physical changes due to sexual maturity, including the external body changes of hair growth, the development of breasts in girls, and the lowering of the pitch of the voice ("breaking") in boys. There is also a growth spurt, increased sweating, and the common onset of the teenager's nightmare—acne! All this is the result of the changing activity of sex hormones, which stimulate the development of the sexual organs leading to the adult ability to reproduce. This is signalled very clearly for females in the onset of the menstrual cycle, while males have the more unpredictable emissions of "wet dreams" and learn to manage having erections. The age at which this happens varies quite widely and has been getting earlier in all industrialized societies, probably due to improved nutrition and health. It begins in girls about two years earlier than in boys. The sex hormones also have emotional effects, which can result in mood changes in girls—for example, at the time of a girl's period—and impulsive or aggressive behaviour in boys. These changes can have significant impacts on all aspects of young people's lives, including their body image and social relationships. These im-

pacts differ between boys and girls and between those who mature earlier or later than their peers.

Mental development

This period sees substantial changes in the cognitive capabilities of young people—and is the reason we expect them to attend school and develop their learning in a wide range of subjects and activities. Thinking about "what if?" is a characteristic development in these years. This is due to the ability to extend logical thinking beyond the real to the possible, or the imagined. Much of their learning is concerned with the understanding of increasingly abstract ideas or concepts, which can be used in a variety of contexts. Take, for example, the understanding of whether an object can float or sink. Young children will focus on a single property such as size or heaviness; older primary-age children can manage to handle the idea that large light objects such as a branch of wood will float and small heavy ones such as a metal ball will sink. A full understanding requires the concept of density—"heaviness compared to size"—and the comparison of the densities of the object and the liquid in which it is immersed. A 14-year-old of average ability can apply this understanding to predict that, or explain why, a steel ball will float in liquid mercury.

Secondary-age children develop their abilities to process information with increasing levels of attention and memory capacity. The amount of knowledge increases greatly, and they can use strategies to solve practical and theoretical problems in contexts ranging from sports to designing to mathematics. These higher-order thinking skills are developed not only through formal teaching, but also through their social interactions in school. Through these relationships, children develop their sense of identity and of responsibility to others, which helps to develop a sense of morality.

Social and emotional development

Adolescence is a key stage for establishing your personal identity. This involves understanding the changes that are happening to you at the present time, interpreting past experiences, and learning of society's expectations for your future. No wonder, then, that adolescence is typically seen as a difficult phase! Relationships with peers are very important in this process, and intense friendships are a common feature. However, these intimate attachments can undergo rapid changes, particularly among younger teenage girls who fall in and out of friendships with confusing frequency!

Same-sex groups, even cliques, dominate the younger teenager's social circle. These may come together to form larger mixed-sex groups and gradually break into smaller mixed-sex groups. Towards the end of this period, individual male–female relationships begin to become important, though "dating" may often begin within looser groups of couples. Some teenagers retain a preference for same-sex friendships.

Relationships with parents are often under strain during middle adolescence, around ages 13 to 15. This is partly a consequence of the adolescents' need to establish their identity, independent of parents. Also their growing confidence in their abilities and physical maturity leads them to believe they should be allowed more independence than their parents think is sensible. Conflict usually arises around the practicalities of keeping safe. When parents point out the dangers of predatory older teenagers, alcohol, drugs, and sex, teenagers protest that they are being treated like children. Parents somehow have to maintain a close, warm engagement with their teenagers, while setting firm, clear limits on what is allowed. Not surprisingly, parental practice varies considerably, not least among different social and ethnic groups. And in the mixed society that most teenagers experience nowadays, this itself can be a source of tension.

Experience of difference

The challenges our disabled children, and we their parents, will meet in this stage are considerable, but, as always, facing up to them and trying to understand them is probably the best strategy! It is helpful to remember the points made above about conflict in the teenage years and to consider how different the inappropriate behaviour of our learning disabled teenagers really is. The first challenge will be that physical and sexual development is not usually delayed unless there is a particular genetic reason. Thus all the physical changes and the hormone-related mood states can be expected, but probably without the accompanying age-related understanding of these changes. It also takes much longer for our disabled teenagers to understand appropriate social and sexual boundaries. This can be a particularly frustrating period for some youngsters, but for others the physical changes occur without too much trouble and are welcomed appropriately as a sign of approaching adulthood. This is most likely to happen when boys and girls have had sex education, carefully tailored to their level of understanding, from an early age. So, for example, the mother of a young girl might start talking about periods from the age of 8 or 9 years, perhaps showing her sanitary pads and how she (mother) puts them on, then letting her see a blood-stained pad and how to dispose of it. Later she could encourage her daughter to wear pads each time her mother has a period, practising for when she has periods herself. When her periods do start, the occasion could be welcomed and celebrated, perhaps by a small grown-up gift such as flowers or jewellery.

Similarly, boys need to know about erections and wet dreams, and both genders need to know about the normality of masturbation and the importance of privacy. If teenagers are masturbating publicly, it is important to try to understand why this is happening. It may simply be an expression of emotional loneliness and signal a need for more hugs and other expressions of love and affection. It could indicate confusion about the sexual feelings the young person is experiencing and just need some consistent and positive management by parents and teachers. Whatever your own attitude towards masturbation, it will be unhelpful to forbid it; rather, the patience and perseverance involved in taking your adolescent child to their room every time they start to masturbate will be time well spent. They will already have learnt that there are many things that are done in private, such as undressing, bathing, and going to the toilet, so emphasize that this is also something to be done in private. In other words, emphasize the inappropriateness of the place rather than the masturbation itself.

Siblings will need particular help at this period, to cope with and understand what will seem very embarrassing behaviour, especially if they are themselves grappling with their own sexual identity.

Puberty is also a critical period for the onset of epilepsy in a significant minority of young people with learning disabilities. Patrick's parents remember the day when he first displayed this additional disabling condition and describe how unfair this seemed to them:

Patrick's school had reported that he had had a couple of unexplained falls. The school doctor had made a referral to a paediatrician for an EEG, but before the appointment we were all going for our usual family get-together at Christmas at the coast. On arrival after supper, when Patrick was tucked up in bed, we asked everyone to keep an extra eye on him. We said he might be starting to have fits and, if he did, what to do.

Next morning was Christmas Eve, a Sunday, and Granny was dressed and all ready to go to the nearby cathedral, but we still had an hour before we needed to leave. Patrick was in the dining-room chatting to his uncle and excited about the prospect of going to the cathedral. From the kitchen we heard a sudden commotion: a cry, a clatter, and then his young cousin calling "Auntie, come quickly". It's dreadful to find your worst fears realized: your son, whose disabilities you've gradually begun to accept, is lying jerking on the floor, breathing with difficulty, turning blue, and frothing at the mouth. There was nothing to be done except turn him into the recovery position, cradle his head, and send for a duvet.

When he came round, after sleeping on the floor for about half-an-hour, Patrick was vaguely displeased about missing going to the cathedral, but we reminded him that we were definitely going to the cathedral on the next day, because that was Christmas Day. We were lucky he hadn't wet himself, because he hates even a trace of dampness. As it was, we could just get gently on with the ordinary business of dressing— and the extraordinary business of trying to learn how to cope with epilepsy as well as autism.

But Patrick was 15, and he did bounce back. He still has infrequent minor symptoms of epilepsy, but it is a real mercy that he is so sublimely unaware of his problems.

Experience of school

The transition from being in the top class of a small primary school, to the lowest class of a large secondary school is often difficult for children. Their teachers do not know them, the curriculum is very different, with many teachers in different rooms, and there are lots of older, potentially threatening students. For these reasons, special schools often take pupils from the complete age range—from primary through to secondary—so there is not such an upsetting change. However, there are advantages in a change of school, as it can give the child a sense of being more grown-up and can provide a wider range of teaching expertise.

Carol and David's mother was clear about what she wanted for David at this point in his education:

David went to our local primary school, and he was accepted and supported there from nursery to Year 6. When it came to leavers' evening, we were moved to tears when the headmaster said that he felt that David had done more for the school than the school had done for him.

So I was determined that David should go to mainstream secondary. After all, it was his "human right", even though he wasn't very bright and couldn't even write!

The secondary school initially accepted him. However, he was never properly supported. Instead of having to relate to only one or two classroom assistants, he had a different one for each lesson and between lessons had to return to the special needs department to "pick up" his next helper. He was always late for lessons and then refused to enter the classroom. He was gradually withdrawn from lessons more and more. I was continually summoned to the school to hear a long list of complaints against him. This was a very negative experience that lasted a whole year. I later discovered from another child that he had been bullied there. The school either did not know, or could not tell me. Everyone, it seems, had put the problems on to David.

It was suggested that he attend a special school twenty miles away. At first I declined—it was much too far and it was unfair to expect David to travel all that way. However, after visiting, I discovered that it was a very special school with wonderful facilities and lovely staff with good attitudes and high expectations.

I can honestly say that, although I was reluctant at first, it was the best thing for David. He is much happier and more relaxed, his speech is improving, and he has nearly lost his stammer! He is really maturing in a less pressured atmosphere.

Difficult choices may therefore need to be made about a change of school. These should be based on assessments by the child's own teachers and other specialists involved such as a paediatrician, therapist, child psychiatrist, or psychologist. Considerations at this stage are similar to those we raised in the previous chapter. How do we balance the particular special needs of our child—which may be best provided somewhere far away and with a segregated group of children with similar needs—with the general social need to have them near us and with their peers, perhaps in a mainstream school? There are additional things to consider with respect to the teenage years. For example, in the light of the importance of peers at this stage, we need to consider the social situation of the school. Are the other pupils those we would want our teenager to identify with? What are the opportunities for spending time with the opposite sex in unstressful situations?

Clearly it is important to get the best information available, both on your child's current progress at school and on the range of provision available. Any reports on your child should be available to you. Schools have a duty to inform parents at least once a year, and many will now use national progress indicators such as the National Curriculum attainment levels. These levels may be inappropriate for those with substantial learning disabilities and so there are now "P-scales" for special education, which identify smaller steps on the way to the national levels (details are available at www.qca.org.uk).

In the transfer from primary school to secondary school, this information will be passed on. The statement of SEN will contain details of the provision to be made. This is helpful in finding the best setting for the child's secondary education. But inevitably, a lot of knowledge and understanding of our children's particular needs can be lost in the change. It is important that we as parents take the opportunity to convey this to the new teachers and therapists. Sometimes the whole person can get lost in the details of the specific needs and the programme of support. For example:

Neil's statement, while accurate in its detailed reports, gave the impression of a shy, quiet, and anxious child, whereas we, as his parents, and his teachers knew him to be sociable and to have a reasonably robust personality, willing to engage with his teachers.

Schools are accountable through a national recording system and through inspections by OFSTED. There is, therefore, a lot of information publicly available on schools' achievements and strengths and weaknesses. Your LEA can tell you where to find it; much is on the Internet.

Jay's parents describe their search for a secondary school place for him:

At the point of secondary schooling we were hoping for Jay's integrated education to continue, but no nearby school was able to take him, and with a bit of sadness we chose a special school for him which with hindsight we feel was the best way forward for him. Our life also became easier, and we felt more supported. He was in his teens now and rebelling at times, which, we thought, could have been very difficult in a mainstream secondary school.

During disruptive periods he could have help more readily now, and he was following a personalized curriculum, unlike when he was in his primary schools. There were also after-school and evening clubs he could join, which helped us all in enlarging our social world, while having fun. At times he had conflicts with his peer group, he was bullied, his behaviour took a nosedive, and so on, but he also made progress there.

Transport is provided if your child has to be educated at a distant school, but this can mean a large part of your child's day can seem like wasted time. The impact of long periods cooped

up in a minibus can have unhelpful consequences during the rest of the day.

> When Neil arrived home from school after an hour's travelling, his behaviour often appeared so manic that the only way to settle him was to sit him in front of the TV for an hour or two. We wondered what use he could be making of the first two hours at school, if he arrived there in a similar state.

His parents commented how different it was when he learnt to come home on the bus on his own.

It may be necessary to consider residential schooling to ensure that the best provision is made. It will be important to obtain as much information as possible before taking such a significant step. You will want to visit to check the particular education provided as well as the wider aspects of care and try to judge your child's response to such a change. You may want to consider the effect on siblings—will this enable them to feel less neglected, by giving some respite from the constant demands of the child with the disability?

You need to be prepared for limited communication about your child's experience once he has gone away. Many of our children will have general communication difficulties or be unable to recall or organize information over the period that we are apart from them. The regular reports seem too infrequent, so it is useful if, every time the child moves between school and home, some written communication should accompany them. This is most likely to be a notebook written in by a teacher or assistant, and also by the parent for the return journey. It can help to capture those day-to-day events that would otherwise be lost.

Here is an extract from a note from Neil's teacher:

"Neil seems to be happy to be back at school and is quite settled again. We've been working on the link-up reading scheme this week—he is doing very well and is reading quite a few words, such as 'bus stop' and 'police car'—a great improvement! On Wednesday we went to the park and took along a boomerang. Neil managed to make it come back! Do come in for a chat again soon!"

This gives parents opportunities to follow up activities and experiences at school—and vice versa. Computer use within special education is developing quite fast, so emails or the exchange of discs could provide a convenient alternative to the notebook.

Computers are also proving an invaluable learning tool for many children with learning disabilities, as David's mother explains:

Our son never used to write. He found it very hard and refused to try—beyond writing his name. Then we discovered the computer. Now he loves writing long lists of Harry Potter characters—quite difficult names—and adding family and friends' names. This now seems to have encouraged him to write by hand—and not just signing birthday cards!

Knowing your changing child

Some teenagers, or even younger children, will have additional challenges to face, which serve to confuse and distort their early understanding of their own and others' sexuality. Sadly the risk of sexual abuse by caretakers is much higher in children with learning disabilities. One of the early signs to suggest a child may have experienced inappropriate or abusive sexual attention is the appearance of sexualized behaviour in the young person. Such behaviour is seen in every special school but is frequently misunderstood or ignored. Indeed, the presence of such behaviour may lead to teachers avoiding discussing gender and sexuality, even though they are an essential part of the curriculum. This behaviour will usually just be due to the children's developing awareness of their own sexuality, in which case gently distracting the child with another activity is fine. Behaviour such as masturbating openly or touching other people's genitals can be so persistent, sometimes even leading to physical harm, that concern should be expressed and specialist advice sought.

When abuse takes place, it is nearly always someone the child knows and trusts and who has persuaded the child not to tell anyone—"it's our secret". It is rare for the abuser to be a stranger. These children's vulnerability to abuse may be linked to their naivety, to a lack of sex education, or to the imbalance in power between themselves and the abuser, and their poor communication skills. The abuser may be an older teenager at school or at the respite care hostel, perhaps someone who him/herself has been abused. However, sometimes adolescent experimentation may be mistaken for abuse, with two young people enjoying the same adventures as other teenagers; perhaps learning disabled young people are more likely to be found out. Distinguishing between what is abusive and what isn't may be rather complicated!

As parents we might conclude that the only solution is to keep our young persons safe at all costs and to restrict their social activities and the range of people they meet. As a parent, however, our task is to support our children's growth and maturity and to help them engage with the wider world, so that they can reach their full potential and lead as full and ordinary lives as is possible. Some risks are inevitable along the way, and part of our job is to recognize any signs of adverse influences so that we can intervene appropriately. If something abusive is suspected, it is vital to ask questions immediately and not to try to handle it alone. Every local authority, church, and voluntary organization should have child and vulnerable-adult protection policies and any concern will immediately be referred to their specially trained child protection officer. Don't challenge the person you suspect yourself. If your child discloses abuse that has just happened, phone the police immediately; don't destroy any evidence—for example, by washing it away.

From an emotional point of view, the most important thing you can do as a parent if your child does make an allegation is to believe him. It is possible to get over such traumatic experiences with the right loving support, although it may be wise to request specialist counselling or therapy to reduce the risk of longer-term consequences. We will also be very concerned to keep our other children and their friends safe. This will demand vigilance in case any of their abusive experiences lead to inappropriate touching or overt abuse of others.

There are some other "secrets", in addition to the secret of sexuality, that parents and teachers may try to keep from young people with learning disabilities, usually in an attempt to protect them from harm. We believe such attempts are usually misguided and have the potential to backfire later! These include the mysteries of ageing, and of death and dying, but also the truth about disability, difference, and continuing dependency.

> Neil had never asked about his difficulties before, although he seemed acutely aware, and sometimes even envious, of his sisters being more able. One evening at supper he suddenly started asking questions about why he couldn't do something. I said that I didn't know how it had happened, but he had been a bit different since he was a baby. Perhaps his brain had been hurt when he was being born and that this made it harder for him to think and to do some things.

Coming to terms with the extent of one's own limitations and impairments is hard for anyone, perhaps especially for a disabled teenager, who wants to be able to do the same things and enjoy the same freedom as older—and even younger—siblings.

> Throughout the time he was a teenager, Neil would protest that he wasn't disabled. He liked disabled people who used wheelchairs and had ideas about helping them, and he showed a real interest in doing this through belonging to his church. He also had ideas about learning to drive a car, and his dad would remind him that he would have to pass a test and that he would have to learn to read to do this. Privately, we worried about his road-safety sense and knew that he had visual perceptual difficulties. These seemed to mean that he couldn't judge the speed or direction of traffic, so that he was unlikely to be able to ride even a bicycle safely on the open road.

As parents we need to manage the changing relationships between all our children, and these are typically a challenge in the teenage years. For teenagers who have a learning disabled sibling, things can get very complicated; their feelings need to be respected and the opportunity given to talk about things, remembering the danger of making them feel guilty for these feelings.

Siblings will have rather different experiences of this period, perhaps depending on their own temperament and whether they are older or younger than their disabled brother or sister. They will probably feel rather neglected by their parents because of the extra dependency needs of the disabled child, and family activities may not be organized around their wishes and abilities. This can lead to the other teenagers in the family spending more time round at their friends' houses rather than inviting friends home. Older siblings may find themselves being asked to do rather more childminding than they want. This is complicated by the fact that this "minding" shows no sign of coming to an end, unlike with other younger siblings who take increasing responsibility for themselves with time. Kirsty's mother recalled:

> Looking back, I think my older children rather missed out, because they had to put so much effort into helping Kirsty. But they were good at socializing with Kirsty and including her when their friends came round.

Free discussion between parents and siblings can help them to accept that their negative feelings are understandable and to feel less guilty. A failure to do this can lead to hidden emotions about tension in the relationships between siblings and their parents, with respect to the disabled family members, as Carol's parents explain:

> We always thought that as a family we coped very well with having two disabled children. We tried to lead as normal a life as possible and not let it affect our other children. We never said anything negative about disability or allowed it to prevent them taking a full part in all their school and social activities.
>
> We were quite shocked when our eldest son was about 20 and we were away together on holiday, having left Carol—our profoundly disabled daughter—in respite care. He cried and said he didn't know how to feel about his disabled sister and felt guilty about his inability to relate to her.

> We tried to reassure him that he mustn't feel guilty, that it was very difficult—even for us—to relate to her when she is unable to respond or even show us that she knows who we are. I told him he mustn't feel in any way responsible for her. I wanted to take all the entire burden away from him. It was profoundly sad.

This is a time when siblings may themselves have questions about the cause of the disability, and they may be wondering about their own parenting potential and whether they might have a disabled child too. Genetic counselling is, of course, a possibility, and in these days of rapid advances in genetic knowledge, advice given to parents in early childhood may be out of date by the time the next generation are contemplating the possibility of having a family.

6

young adults

Typical expectations of young adults

This chapter covers the stage of life associated with the final years of full-time education and beyond, into employment or similar activity. For most young adults, it is a time of choice. Society and the educational system may at last be ready to recognize their maturity and increasing ability to take their own decisions about their futures.

The physical, emotional, and mental developments of adolescence, described in the previous chapter, will typically be completed during this period. For example, some boys may still experience growth spurts and other physical changes until around the age of 18 years. Mental abilities and capacity also continue to develop, particularly with respect to handling abstract ideas, developing thinking strategies, and analysing different viewpoints and conflicting evidence.

By the end of adolescence, most young adults will have developed a clear understanding of their own identity. This will include elements that are quite individual, such as personality and body image, and special abilities—say, in sport or arts. However, much of young adults' views of themselves will be determined in relation to others. This is the result of the particular social and cultural world in which they are growing up.

The final years of schooling are dominated by examinations for qualifications such as GCSE and GCE "A" level. Students have choices of which courses to take, but they and their advisers are influenced not only by individual preferences, but also by the competitive nature of examinations and the fact that entry to higher education, training, or employment depends on how one person's examination grades compare to others. At the end of schooling, each young person needs to have chosen their next step. Individuals will vary greatly in the confidence with which they do this. But each person's decisions will be influenced by where they consider they "fit" in society, and by what their personal hopes and dreams are, based on how they understand the adult world.

In their later years of schooling, students are increasingly introduced to the world of work. There will be workplace visits and placements for a week or two. The curriculum subjects are expected to show how any learning could be useful in future employment. Many students will take courses at the age of 16+ that combine time in college and time in employment. Students also take their own part-time jobs, from the young newspaper deliverer to the Saturday shop assistant. All of these activities can support the young adults' growing self-esteem and aspiration for autonomy, as well as ready cash to support their leisure activities. They also may provide formative experiences on which to draw when making important decisions about the future. For example, a period of being bored in a shop or office assistant role can be a strong motivation to keep on studying to improve one's opportunities for a better job.

Young adults also define themselves through their choice of social activities. By this age, most will have considerable freedom to choose these, though of course their availability varies greatly depending on where they live. Parental concerns about the vulnerability of their offspring may be lessening but are rarely absent, even when the young person lives mainly away from home—for example, at college. As adulthood approaches, most young people achieve a more equal relation-ship with their parents, though the challenges of their future ambitions (or apparent lack of!) can be difficult for parents who may be facing their own mid-life challenges.

Relationships with the opposite sex become very important at this age and provide important opportunities for expressing one's choice, defining one's identity, and provoking parental anxiety! For those who recognize that their sexual preferences are for the same sex, these aspects will be even more pro-nounced, even in a society that is much more accepting of gay and lesbian relationships than it was previously. Sexual intimacy is common and widely accepted, but the risks are not always recognized. The incidences of sexually transmitted diseases are increasing rapidly, and the UK has a very high teenage-preg-nancy rate, by international standards. Becoming a young mum is one way of defining one's adult identity, but when unplanned it can be a rather sudden lesson in the implications of one's actions for the future.

Making the most of being different

Young adults of whatever ability want to feel more independent in the way they live their lives, whether this is in education, employment, or another activity. This is a continuing concern for all parents, but how can we manage this with our more vulnerable offspring? Careful attention to social life can be very helpful. Building on previous success is always a good idea. For example, an activity such as a sports team, scouts, or guides may have an older counterpart group, in which some of the same people are involved. Friendships can be maintained, and the knowledge of particular needs is more readily available. But they may want to engage in something different. Most local authorities will have programmes run by social services and can provide details of other agency provision. These can be as diverse as "drop-in" clubs enabling young people to meet and make friends, residential holidays where deeper involvement in activities and in relationships can be fostered, or specific-interest groups that can provide continuing opportunities for development such as music or drama.

Participation in these kinds of activities can help these young adults feel less different from their peers, whether the group they join is special or mixed, because they are doing similar things as their siblings, or people that they see on the TV. In doing this we may support them in developing their relationships with us, in the family, by bringing back their own different experiences from the outside world.

However, the choice of social activities and opportunities to develop close relationships are more limited for learning disabled young adults.

Neil had had a bad day. His drop-in club was closed, and he had found it hard to accept this. At supper his younger sister was talking about going to a youth club. He was angry—"she's not old enough to go to a club. I go to clubs—not Eleanor". He threw his food on the floor and, later that evening, stripped her bedroom door of all its decorations and threw them out of the window.

Jay fared rather better at having a full and varied programme of leisure activities. He made very good progress in sports, both at school and in out-of-school clubs.

In the evenings he attends two swimming clubs and one sports club most weeks. We often provide transport to and from these, while occasionally he goes by minicab or, rarely, by bus under our supervision. We also take him to speedway and stockcar meetings in a nearby stadium when he wants. He likes to go for ten-pin-bowling evenings with people from his centre. Less often he goes to disco or quiz nights at his centre.

During weekends he sometimes goes to the cinema or restaurants with us. He often prefers to eat in a cafe or a burger bar by himself while we wait outside. He also likes going to a library or a pub evening with us. He loves going on holidays abroad with us, and at times he goes away with his swimming team—for example, he will be going to Glasgow next year for a week for special Olympics with his team. He loves music and television.

Patrick's father describes the arrangements his family make to be able to enjoy the short periods of time they are able share with him, now that he lives in his own home.

When Patrick is on holiday with us, we know him and his strange ways so well that we unconsciously arrange the world around him. We avoid all those elements of everyday life that so disturb his autistic mind; or, at least, if they are unavoidable, we prepare him for the reality and constantly reassure him and try to overcome his anxiety about towns, noises, new people, buildings, babies, and especially ice-cream vans. All this is second nature to us, his parents, and to some extent to his brother and sister. These rearrangements are less exhausting than they used to be, but that is because they happen less often or, perhaps more accurately, because we only plan to see Patrick in places and at times when the rearrangements can be minimized. Despite all our efforts, however, disasters still happen. Patrick's twenty-first-birthday treat to the London Eye came to an abrupt halt with wild and uncontrollable shrieking and tears when faced by six ice-cream vans in a row! The taxi driver was understanding and drove us on to a quiet car park where Patrick could calm down, watching trains cross the Thames to Charing Cross. He finally got to see Big Ben from the London Eye a few months later—at twilight, when all the ice-cream vans had gone home!

Engaging with the wider world

The world can offer a bewildering range of options to parents at this stage. Further education may involve moving from school to college; college may offer work-related courses, access to employment schemes, and part-time placements in work. Social activities need to be arranged in ways that are increasingly separate from school or college. And then there is the need to think seriously about the long term—in particular, about working and living options. How independent can *our* young person be in the future?

Schools and colleges

The education system of schools and colleges is organized so that students make important choices at age 16 years and again at 18 or 19. Within special education it is recognized that these ages should not be so critical: schools run programmes beyond age 16, and colleges increasingly accept students on a wide range of courses at all ages. However, parents and their children will be aware that other young people are making choices at these ages, and this can lead to pressure to take decisions prematurely. Planning for post-age 16 should begin for a child with special educational needs at age 14 through the preparation of a transition plan, as part of the Year 9 Annual Review, and the plan should be updated each year. It should address questions about whether education after age 16 is appropriate and, if so, where. Starting at this age is intended to give everyone concerned time to take sensible decisions. The statement of SEN will be continued if the young adult continues in school after 16. If the young person is going to move to another LEA-maintained institution, then the transition plan should be amended by 15 February in the year of transfer. If provision continues in education or training outside the LEA responsibility, such as a further education college, then the Connexions Service will arrange assessments. Personal advisers for people with learning disabilities are part of the local Learning and Skills Council. They provide information about learning and training opportunities and help young people think about their future. If the young person leaves school or college for employment, then the statement will cease to operate as the LEA will no longer be responsible.

A further education college may offer a wider range of courses than does a school, and enrolment can offer the young person with a learning disability the motivation of doing something he has a particular interest in. It is also encouraging to be joining something more adult, rather like your peers. But a college can be a very busy environment compared to a special school, or even a mainstream school, and this can make it hard to cope. In choosing a change like this, parents should look to see what support a college offers, such as small tutor groups, perhaps with a separate base for the "special needs" students, to provide a more manageable social environment. In recent years, colleges have given more attention to the needs of those with learning disabilities to provide inclusive learning. As with schools, funding may be available for extra support to enable a student to carry out their Individual Learning Plan, though this can be more difficult in adult education classes.

The particular needs of the young person may be best met in a residential setting. This is always a difficult choice, as we have noted earlier. At this age there are particular issues. If the placement is related to employment—for example, living in a rural setting with agricultural and horticultural activities—then future life patterns are beginning to be established. These routines might be difficult to connect with for a family that lives in a town. As parents we may find, without planning it, that our child is being trained for a life apart from us. Of course, in the past this was the normal expectation for children such as ours: at some stage in their lives, their needs were considered to be best provided for in residential institutions, often large and remote, where families would be merely visitors. This degree of segregation is not something that many of us would accept today, but some of these attitudes may linger in society and continue to need to be challenged.

On the other hand, it is still considered normal for many school-leavers to be resident at a college or university for three or more years to get a degree. After this, they may return home for a while until they are established in employment. Our son or daughter with a learning disability may not understand this. When they go away to college, they may think it is permanent and feel rejected by their family. Or, instead, they may not see this as a stepping-stone to a separate adult life but assume that when college is finished they will return home for good.

Transition to adult life

The government policy, in England, for people with learning disabilities is set out in *Valuing People* (2001). It established Learning Disability Partnership Boards to ensure, among other things, that young adults themselves have a say in planning services to meet their needs. This can be seen as a radical step in treating them as adult consumers rather than as disabled recipients.

In helping to consider their options, the Connexions Service has a key role, following on from their responsibility for transition planning while the young person is still at school. The final-year's review should include input from advisers from local colleges, employment agencies, and possibly social services. Connexions personal advisers should be available to work with young adults until they are 25 years old, advising on the support needed during transitions in education and training. Social services are responsible for making sure there are good links between children's and adults' services for people with learning disabilities. The GP should be able to ensure that each young adult develops a personal health action plan. This could include advice on staying healthy and how to use the NHS.

The *Valuing People* policy recognizes that its aspirations will require considerable changes in attitudes on the part of the non-disabled population, not least in the field of employment. It proposes that people with learning disabilities should play a role in bringing about these changes. One example of this is that several members of the National Task Force charged with overseeing these changes are people with learning disabilities, including the co-chair.

Other possible job opportunities will involve training those whose work will involve them with people with learning disabilities, such as educators, social workers, or doctors. Gary Butler is employed as a trainer at St George's Hospital Medical School in London. One aspect of his work is to teach medical students. He has no formal qualifications, but he has been a frequent patient in the hospital since he was a small boy, and he has strong views about what the doctors of the future need to know about people with learning disabilities. What he says about this work is both profoundly important for future health care for people with learning disabilities, and also refreshingly familiar, as he faces a common teacher problem:

> Sometimes the teaching is hard. Especially when the students don't say anything. I ask myself "Am I wasting my time talking to this lot?" I need to wake them up a bit more.

a new kind of
trainer

How to Develop the Training Role for People with Learning Disabilities

By Christine Owen, Gary K. Friel and Sheila Hollins
Photographs by Paul Stuart

I hope my teaching will change how they think about people with learning disabilities. So that we are seen in a more positive light, so people don't think straight away that we won't understand. [*A New Kind of Trainer*, 2004]

Gary's experience suggests that the kind of work that trainers are needed for includes:

- Helping others know about the issues affecting people with learning disabilities in their lives
- Making information easier to understand
- Giving advice on how to listen
- Giving advice on how to include people with learning disabilities.

Those people who are most disabled, and most in need of support, are least likely to continue with any education or training and least likely to have any experience of the world of work. This is a group that the Learning Disability Partnership Board needs to work particularly hard to include, perhaps trying new methods of advocacy and certainly also consulting family carers.

Knowing your changing young adult

So what experiences of college and work did our five children who are now adults have, as they reached the end of their schooling? All of them found the transition difficult to negotiate, although in rather different ways.

Jay left school at 16, but we were lucky in that he could stay on till 19 in the college part of his school. He could learn about independence while continuing contact with the people he knew there. Then we found that he could not be accepted in any local college for further education, so we applied for a residential college just outside London. We were very happy that he was accepted there. One of us took him to the college on Monday morning and brought him home on Friday evening. We also visited him on Wednesday evenings and rang him for a brief chat every other evening of the working week.

Jay enjoyed it more than he missed home or us. He could practise some of the things he had learnt earlier, and also learnt some new things. After two years we applied for him to live in a local group home and were again happy that he was accepted. He has been living there for almost three years now. Until a few months ago he wanted to come home every weekend, like he used to do before, but that has now reduced. We still see him almost every day, but the duration varies a lot.

Jay regularly goes to a day centre, which is at a stone's throw distance from his home, and he walks there by himself. There he has a weekly timetable of activities, which he has chosen. He has a key worker who coordinates his activities. This person meets Jay with us, his social worker, and his home key worker at least once a year to review his timetable and overall progress. He is interested in catering, gardening, recycling, car washing, vacuuming, and so on but still needs training if he is going to work in one of these jobs.

Jay prefers to be friends with staff and parents more than his contemporaries. He does enjoy the company of other swimmers in his swimming clubs but can't be really friends with them. He is forever talking about having a girlfriend (and two children!) but mostly chooses staff to be his girlfriend, which doesn't work, and he doesn't know why! He knows so many people and gets very excited when he sees a familiar person in a new place. He has a very good memory for names, which impresses most people, but his repetitive and forceful talking style puts people off. He also is easily jealous.

At 16, Kirsty left the "delicate" school, where she had made good academic progress, at the suggestion of the head teacher, as a group of girls in her class were teasing her and generally making life miserable. She became quiet and didn't want to go to school. She started at the local special school for children with severe learning disabilities and settled in immediately, knowing many of the other teenagers from her swimming club. Her academic work gradually went downhill, and at 17 she moved to a Link Course at the local further education college and enrolled on a vocational access course. Going to college was initially enjoyable, but it was a busy place and her group did not mix with the other students. Her tutors were very pleased with her progress. She also enjoyed a dancing class elsewhere, relying on her parents for transport. All the young people had Down's syndrome, and as Kirsty had attended ballet classes from age 6 to 10, she was very capable. This improved her self-confidence a lot and enlarged her friendships.

In 2002, after years of knee pain, Kirsty had an operation for tibial tubercle realignment, which has reduced though not removed the problem. Now she is in her twenties and has a varied occupational portfolio. She does paid office work one day each week and has a training work placement in a café.

Throughout these years Kirsty's older siblings were also growing up, taking exams, and bringing friends home. They were having boyfriends and girlfriends and eventually getting married and having children! Kirsty was sad each time one of them left home and used to ask them to come back. Now she visits them, and sometimes says she wishes she could live like that. Later she will say she couldn't cope with a baby, and anyway she wants to stay home with us.

At 17, Patrick went to live in a 52-week-a-year residential school, and his parents were expecting that his adult life would be away from the family home. On Patrick's eighteenth birthday, his father wrote about his feelings now that he and the rest of the family had less frequent contact with him.

"We knew him to be there in the company of strangers— well-meaning strangers who were always free with their information about Patrick when we spoke and who were clearly taken by his winning ways, but they were certainly strangers to me. I knew he was being cared for well, but that could not dispel the images of locks on all the doors, the assault-resistant toilets, or the loud speech, the shocks, and the unsettling ways of all the other students at the school. By now I have seen many special schools, and I am grateful that Patrick is clearly at one of the better ones. But it is not the world of our family, and my heart shrinks with this awareness each time we unpack his case on a visit home and we come across unlikely clothing—as if he is an orphan, without roots. And when friends and colleagues ask 'How's Patrick getting on?' I cannot bring myself to speak of the detail of the school which is his home for nearly fifty weeks of the year. This is partly to spare them the embarrassment of not knowing how to react to this kind of stark information, and partly not to have to relive the anguish myself."

When Patrick was 19, he left this school for a supported-living project with other young people. This was unsuccessful, and after a few months at home Patrick was then placed in a "solo" supported-living project.

When Patrick went to live in his own flat, he was naturally rather worried about it all. Life in the last few years had not been easy, and he wasn't sure what lay in store and what was expected of him. Although he had difficulty understanding the world, he could read, and written information always helped him sort out his thoughts. This is what we wrote down for Patrick on the day he started in his new flat. We used some of his own (rather odd) phrases to try and make everything clear.

"*Whitfield House*

"Today is Sunday, May 20th—cousin Emily's birthday!

"My new flat is ready at Whitfield House, in Sharringford village.

"So I will be living in a peaceful village, in a flat on my own. I will have friendly staff to help me. They will keep me company, and help me do things, and keep me safe when we are out and about.

"At first it will be new, and I don't know it very well yet.

"But I will have my Victor [his special soft toy—a black cat] with me, and my music and my books, I will have all the ordinary things to do: like bathroom jobs, to be a smart young man, helping with chopping, and laying the table, and drying-up.

"There will also be times to go out for fresh air and exercise. And there will be trips to interesting places. Everyone at Whitfield House will try to understand me, so I am not in trouble with my life, so I can grow up to be happy in my life.

"God bless Patrick!"

At 18, Neil became a student at a residential college for young adults with moderate learning disabilities.

The college was doubtful about Neil's suitability, initially thinking he was too able and then that his needs were too complex. As usual he was rather a puzzle, and staff failed to really engage with him. Trying to find out what Neil thought about it all was a challenge to us.

A note made by his father at the time said:

"He has remained fairly quiet during this holiday period. We had a long and painfully slow conversation tonight to try to identify what might be wrong. He said that college is too far away. We are not sure if this is a reaction to the last train-journey home having an unscheduled timetable change. Or whether this is just his way of saying he doesn't like college! We talked about what he wanted to happen next in his life, and asked if he was expecting to come back to live at home. He replied 'probably' . . . a favourite word which usually seems to mean 'yes, definitely'! We reminded him that his sister didn't return to live at home after she finished at college, and we suggested a trial stay at a group home which we had visited many times as friends of the residents. He seemed amenable to this."

Neil did go to live in a group home where five other adults of varying ages were living, but group living was not ideal for him and there were many arguments, finally culminating in a request for him to leave. We asked Circles Network for advice, and a "facilitator" came to meet him and his family. Neil thought about who he would like to help him think about his future and to help him to make his dreams come true. His first Circle meeting soon took place, and he was able to express his hopes about doing more acting—his favourite activity at school—and about his wish to get engaged to his girlfriend and to live in his own home not far from us. His own home was made possible through a shared-ownership option with a housing association. We got excellent advice from the Housing Options website [see Resources]. His rent and support were paid by the housing department using a funding stream called "Supporting People", and his benefits were sufficient to meet his daily living expenses. The social services department had modernized its day services and introduced some work-based daily activity programmes, which included a theatre group, so now he "works" as an actor and has achieved two of his dreams.

It seems that young people with profound and multiple learning disabilities have fewer choices at times of transition—though perhaps it would be more accurate to say that their parents have fewer choices, as Carol's mother explains:

We did not seem to experience much in the way of transition with our daughter Carol. One day she was in school—a local special school—and she received some limited help from children's services: some respite care and a nurse twice weekly from the health services. Then she left school and was at home full time with no support whatsoever.

We discovered she should now be under "adult services", but these did not seem to be forthcoming.

The school then agreed that Carol should stay on at school another term, until alternative arrangements could be made. There followed regular meetings with numerous professionals, but nothing appropriate was available, despite a long assessment process. There were no resources available in the area for a profoundly multi-disabled young person. She could not attend college; also, she could not attend the local day services and respite care home, as they could not cater to her very special needs.

Everyone assumed that we would want supported living for her. They didn't seem to understand that we wanted Carol to stay at home and receive full day support from a suitable day service. It seems as if it was all or nothing: full time away in a care home—although there was nothing suitable available—or no support at home.

I became a full-time carer and was completely housebound. Eventually I persuaded them to arrange for a few hours of Crossroads Care in order to allow me out of the house to do some shopping.

It took a change of social worker and a year of struggling to eventually organize Direct Payments and Independent Living Funds in order to buy in the services she needs. Direct Payments are an arrangement where disabled persons "employ" a personal assistant of their own choice at hours that suit them, within the provisions of the transition plan or care plan agreed by social services. Also, I have now been able to arrange live-in help!

It is still not altogether satisfactory, but it is better than nothing. I am looking to the charity Sense to provide an Intervener Service—a full-time carer during the day and a range of alternative activities suitable to the needs of a severely multi-disabled young person who is deaf and blind. Also, we are looking for some appropriate respite care.

Maybe we were not fully prepared for the future or had not thought about what would happen when Carol left school. We had not expected her to live very long. We never imagined she would make it to adulthood, or that we would be having to make plans for her future and ours! How difficult it is to let go!

It is important to keep on listening and planning as the years unfold. Someone in the family, as well as a care manager from social services, needs to keep up to date with new opportunities and to be familiar with support systems such as Supported Living, Supported Employment, and Direct Payments.

7

mental and emotional
health and behaviour

Problems and solutions

One recurring theme throughout this book is that each child—but especially each learning disabled child—is unique, and we have to become the "experts" on our own child. We still need advice, but we as parents are the full-time experts: the paediatrician, child psychologist, or psychiatrist are part-time experts for our child, and so they can only see a small part of the story. These "part-time" experts will never have seen a child exactly the same as ours, so we must be the advocate and interpreter. Sometimes child psychiatry services have taken the ill-informed view that if the child is disabled, then nothing can be done, because the impairment itself cannot be cured! This means they will lack practice in applying ideas about how children with learning disabilities gain control over their thoughts and fears and begin to make sense of the real, objective world.

Common problems seen by children's specialists—such as feeding and sleeping difficulties, separation anxiety, or temper tantrums—have well-rehearsed solutions, but these are harder to apply when a child is developmentally delayed. Specialists will try to understand the history of a particular problem. What exactly happened when? When was the problem first noticed? Did anything change around that time? Did anything happen to upset the baby or child? For example, was there a new babysitter, did it coincide with the birth of a new baby in the family, or was mother unwell? These attempts to understand will require even more patience on the part of the specialist when the child has complex problems that have been ongoing for a long time—exceptionally good memories are invaluable for parents! Keeping careful notes or a diary of day-to-day events is probably the best way for busy parents to remember enough details.

Typical expectations

Children are not born with any understanding of how the world works, and no child has the mental ability to make sense of his relationships with his parents for several years. Selma Fraiberg called these early years "the magic years", meaning that children construct a fantasy world, over which they struggle to gain control and which is gradually replaced by a world that contains some certainties. They have "tested out" this real world and have found that the adults in the real world are reliable and reassuring figures, who have helped them to gain some self-control and a conscience. They begin to develop healthy strategies to deal with conflict and anxiety, and they are not afraid to try out new things and to take some risks. In this way they grow into adulthood, confident in themselves and able to make intimate relationships. There will have been many hurdles along the way, but, with steady support from family and teachers, these will have been overcome. Some difficulties are harder than others—for example, if a parent or sibling dies, or if a sibling has a severe disability—but even coping with these experiences can bring new learning opportunities.

Facing up to difference

How are these steps negotiated, and how do children with learning disabilities fare, faced with the same tasks? Will the world understand them enough if their timetable for achieving these steps is very out of sync with that for other children? There is a risk that their emotional development will be placed second to their intellectual development, especially given the high value our society puts on academic achievement. In fact, the two need to go hand in hand—for example, the mastery of language and acquisition of knowledge can also help a child to establish the difference between reality and fantasy.

Once again, we need to remind ourselves that our child can only proceed at the pace that his development and mental ability will allow. As parents we cannot provide an ideal environment, but we can help our children to develop their inner resources and learn to overcome their fears. We will, of course, tailor our approach for their particular personality and, hopefully, have the confidence to say what will or won't work for our child.

Engaging with the wider world

People who do not know our children often say they are difficult and stubborn, because they don't know how best to interact with them. They get cross with them and tell them off. The child/adult can get frightened and display aggressive behaviour—and they wonder why. Wouldn't anyone become very frustrated if no one understood what they were saying or what they wanted? If you didn't know what was happening and someone tried to manhandle you, wouldn't you resist or lash out, too?

David really likes routine and doing things in the same sequence. It helps him understand the world better. It is important to prepare him well in advance about what is happening and go over it several times to let it sink in.

If you spring something on him, he will often refuse to cooperate and can become very stubborn—no amount of cajoling or getting cross will make him acquiesce. However, if you remind him over a few days or write it down like a timetable of events, "on Saturday we are going to a party", and then break it down into stages—getting a shower, getting changed into party clothes, going in the car, and so on—it helps him to understand and then he cooperates. Also, it helps to talk about events afterwards, to help to clarify, understand, and remember.

The wider world includes medical and other specialist appointments, which may be in unfamiliar places, cause considerable anxiety, and involve quite an expedition. Patrick's mother explains how one such trip worked out.

Today was going to be different from ordinary days in his holidays from school: we had to go on a train for an appointment with a specialist dentist in London. Patrick walked through the station concourse with bright eyes, eagerly anticipating the excitement of the journey. But his hands were clamped over his ears to mute the worst of the noise around him. Once on the train he was in seventh heaven, taking intense pleasure in the novelty of speeding through the countryside—for once not in a car, but with space to move about and an unrestricted view. Enjoying that slight swaying and rhythm of jiggety-can and the sudden shock of the dark of the tunnels.

After the dentist, we rattled along in the underground train, which Patrick adored. Climbing to the top of the dome of St Paul's with 11-year-old Patrick was great, and so much more fun than going to the local park would ever be. Since it was proving such fun to be in London, why not go and visit Patrick's cousin who was working in Harrods?

Patrick saw it before I did—he let out an ear-splitting shriek and ran straight across the road towards the glass doors of the store. His shriek told me he had seen an ice-cream van. He was absolutely terrified, screaming and crying, with those huge tears that jump out of his eyes. I'd manoeuvred him against the sidewall of the entrance, so rather startled passers-by could get on with their surge into the high temple of shopping. I didn't know what to do: the stupid ice-cream van outside was parked on double yellow lines, with no driver in sight, so we couldn't go back. Patrick's cousin, lovely though she was, would be mortified by this display of totally asocial behaviour, and it would hardly do her reputation any good to be linked with us today.

I was past caring about the glares of affronted shoppers, who clearly thought we were an outrageous spectacle (maybe some looked at us sympathetically but didn't know how to help). I was running out of tissues for the stream of tears and snot.

Two very large security guards approached through the shoppers: "Is there any way we can help you, Madam?" "I wish there were, but I'm honestly not sure what you can safely do." I should have thought to ask them to pick up the ice-cream van and remove it from Patrick's field of vision; at least that wouldn't scratch their eyes or bite their ears off if they touched it. I clearly couldn't stay there, so I hugged Patrick tight and lifted him just enough to stagger out of the doors and across Hans Crescent, past the ice-cream van and then fifteen yards further to be well clear. I put Patrick down, and he wiped his hands across his wet eyes and said "Wasn't I a brave boy?" so sweetly, as though he'd just emerged from a ghost train at a fair, and managed it all by himself. I fancied an intravenous gin but thought the next best thing would be to cross over into Hyde Park, where we might recover, away from the relentless shopping public and traffic. At least my back had not been damaged again.

Suddenly home seemed like a really good idea: "Patrick, shall we go on the underground, and then on the train home?" "Yeah, underground, that good idea, AND train, and then I see my dad and tell him all about St Paul's."

Anxiety is a useful and intuitive reaction to danger, and infants usually move quite quickly from experiencing surprise or shock at unfamiliar sounds and experiences to being able to anticipate separations and experience anticipatory anxiety. There is evidence that anticipating danger or a separation can help one to cope better. We return to this important point later in the chapter.

There are some necessary mental tasks involved in achieving a sense of self and a measure of self-control. First, imagination may play a major part. For example, during the "magic years", most children will experience some fears and have nightmares about ogres and tigers, for example, in their bedroom. Imaginary companions and imaginary play can provide one way to tame these "bogies" and also to help parents understand something of the fears being experienced. Children who lack the language to talk about "ogres and tigers" may miss out on the reassuring understanding of their parents. To be most helpful, parents need to deal with both imagined and real "bogies" in an open and honest way and support their children to do the same. It is not the presence or absence of such fears, but the child's solution to them that will matter as he faces difficulties throughout life. Knowledge can help, but knowledge is harder to acquire for our children and may require imaginative and creative explanations. Usually these early childhood fears have been mastered by the time a child starts school. If fantasized dangers are reinforced by real dangers, such as might be posed by an angry or violent parent, then the child will find it more difficult to overcome his fantasies. Sometimes imagined threats invade the child's real life too, and become a fixed part of his inner world.

Good mental health demands a well-functioning mind, which is able to maintain a balance between our inner needs and others' demands, and we do this by adapting to and integrating our learning and experiences. We want both to be loved and to avoid our parent's disapproval, and this is how conscience begins to develop. We may have a wish that is contrary to our conscience or our parents' standards, and we will need a strong ego to reach a satisfactory solution to such a conflict. If a solution cannot be reached, we will have to find a compromise, and this can take up a lot of our emotional energy.

The development of conscience

Some may question whether conscience can develop in a child of lower intellectual ability, but our view is that, for many, this is a matter of degree and adequate time being allowed. Often it is life experience and good-enough parenting that will help our children achieve quite extraordinary advances in mental stability and maturity, despite their intellectual limitations. Thus we may see an adult aged 25 achieving advances more typically seen in a child of 5 or 6. These advances will have real significance for his life as an adult and are to be welcomed, however late they may seem.

Perhaps it is also worth mentioning that many young people with learning disabilities develop a deep spirituality and aware-ness of the presence of God in their lives. This can be nurtured by family members ensuring that they are truly welcome mem-bers of their own faith community.

Our disabled children may still be struggling with childish fears when they reach adulthood, and this can lead to misdiagnoses of mental illness. Perhaps more importantly, a child who throughout childhood has struggled with unresolved and irresolvable fears may develop problematic personality traits, or experience crippling states of anxiety and panic, that will limit their lifestyle in adulthood. A child or young person who feels helpless may develop personality traits involving fearful submission in all contact with others. A child who feels threatened on all sides and is always on guard may develop aggressive personality traits. Personality and relationship difficulties such as these do respond to psychotherapeutic treatment, but, as always, a stitch in time saves nine—the earlier psychologically informed help is offered the better.

Sorting out the physical from the emotional

Sometimes it is difficult to know whether a particular behavioural response is due to a physical cause, perhaps pain or a sensory loss, or has some other message to give. David's mother wonders if he really is deaf—something that is very common in Down's syndrome:

All the tests showed that David had a substantial hearing loss. He did have a problem with glue ear and had several grommets and T-tubes fitted. Hearing aids were not successful—he refused to wear them. However, I was never convinced that he was deaf. Sometimes he failed to respond, but this seemed to be by choice. If I spoke quietly to him from across the room, he understood. He doesn't like a lot of noise and cannot understand general conversation. He needs to be spoken to more on an individual basis, using simple words and phrases.

Another big problem was the runny nose he had for years from when he was born until about age 15 years. It was very difficult and embarrassing to be constantly blowing his nose—he just couldn't get the hang of it himself. There was pressure to have a medical intervention, which we resisted, and now he seems to have grown out of it.

Feeling rejected

A fear that many learning disabled people have is that they were not wanted in the first place, that society would prefer them to have been aborted before birth and, given any chance, would deny them life-saving treatment now or seek other means to annihilate them. There are occasional high-profile stories in the news of desperate, inadequately supported parents who suffocated their profoundly disabled child or adult family member because they could not bear the pain of it all any longer. However much sympathy one might have for their plight, euthanasia does not seem to us to offer a solution; rather, it further devalues the life of severely disabled people and increases the feelings of worthlessness some people have about themselves and their fear about their own safety. As parents of severely disabled children, we have probably all "wished" our child dead at some point in their lives—and then felt desperately guilty for feeling such thoughts. It is hard to reconcile these deeply felt and painful thoughts with our own anger and disappointment with other people who seem not to value our child enough. The associated stigma, and the revulsion some people apparently feel towards severely disabled people, sometimes leads to thuggish behaviour on the part of other members of society. This may arise from fear of such difference. When our most vulnerable family member is hurt by a thug—whether through unkind words, by excluding them from membership of a group, or by bullying or actual physical assault—then we will feel that hurt as well.

Sometimes we may feel that service providers do not have our child's best needs at heart, and we may be frustrated at their lack of willingness to devote scarce resources to help or support our disabled child. Sometimes it is we who have become stuck and unable to move on, unable to stand back and see that new opportunities or different approaches are worth trying. In many ways this emphasizes yet again the importance of strong partnerships with professional advisors. We need advisors who do not have their own axe to grind, but who are there to be a guide or facilitator, to support us in navigating in this foreign world, where adjustments are constantly needed to enable our child find a good-enough "fit" with his particular special needs. There are risks of misdiagnosis if wider social cues are not listened to, as Patrick's parents found out:

After leaving school, Patrick lived in his own flat, supported by a team of carers from a care agency contracted by the social services department. The health team wondered if Patrick was depressed. Certainly his behaviour seemed to indicate someone who was not happy with his life. His behaviour towards many of his support workers was frequently violent; he became obsessed with writing notes to himself and then sticking them up all over his bedroom wall; he watched a lot of unsuitable television; he refused to get involved in most suggested activities. The team asked the care staff to monitor certain aspects of Patrick's life so that the health professionals could analyse their observations about sleep patterns, aggressive behaviour, etc. in order to make a diagnosis. Patrick seemed to move from being someone supported to live in his own flat to being a patient whom the professionals were trying to diagnose and treat.

It was all well-meaning, but none of the key people had a real knowledge of Patrick. None of the professionals seemed to be asking if this was the right setting for Patrick. If they had asked us, we would have told them that at weekends and on holiday Patrick was his usual self, pottering along, often singing, and willing to participate with encouragement in a fairly wide range of activities. It was a measure of how unhappy he was with the arrangements in his new flat that Patrick began to tell us that he didn't wish to go back there. Normally he has great difficulty in finding language to express his feelings.

So with the support of social services we arranged for him to move into his own house with supporters whom we recruited and trained. He receives Direct Payments (funding directly from social services) to enable us to purchase, on his behalf, the kind of support that works for him. We set up a Care Trust to administer the funds and recruit support workers on the basis of how well they relate to Patrick. He regards his new house as "home". Outings in the previous setting had become limited to a drive to the nearest shop for Patrick to buy a magazine and a Coke; exercise had been the walk to the shop. Now Patrick has some form of sporting activity nearly every day, and with support he goes to folk groups, visits the cinema, plays the organ in local churches, buys vegetables and meat from local farms, enjoys ten-pin bowling and swimming, and helps around the house. Once a week Patrick goes to friends' houses to watch his favourite videos.

He may have been depressed before or just unhappy—but we knew that the answer to the problem wasn't medication: it was a different place and style of living that was needed, with a different kind of support.

Facing separation and death

Earlier in this chapter we wrote about the useful role of anticipatory anxiety in preparing for separation and danger and the importance of knowledge to help us to grasp the difference between fantasy and reality. One of the challenges to be faced is whether we will have the courage to deal openly with major separations and death, or whether we will try to hide these painful realities from our children.

One day our children will experience death for the first time, usually of an older relative, but disabled children are also more likely to know a peer who dies—for example, from epilepsy or heart disease. While the life expectancy of people with learning disabilities is catching up with the general population, there is still an increased risk of earlier death—for example, because of associated health problems, but also because of the greater difficulty in making accurate diagnoses in people with less well developed verbal skills or who have very limited understanding of how their bodies work.

When someone dies, a common reaction is not to tell children or adults with learning difficulties. Perhaps this is because death is hard to explain, but the reluctance also probably arises from a fear of their unknown reaction. There are resources available in pictures to support information and counselling about such difficult life experiences in the Books Beyond Words series edited by one of the authors of this book. Our experience is that it is worth taking the time and thought needed to allow the young person to play as full a part in the events surrounding a death as they feel able to. This could include visiting the dying person in hospital, seeing the body after death, choosing music or flowers for the funeral, choosing

a memento and photograph of the person who has died, and so on, according to the customs of their faith and culture. They will probably show signs of upset, and this may be expressed behaviourally and be difficult for family members to manage when they themselves are also grieving. However, by being included they will have a chance to learn how other people manage their feelings of grief, and they will be able to cry and remember with others in a culturally appropriate way. The nonverbal aspects of funeral rituals are helpful to most people and will be especially helpful to people who cannot seek solace in words.

The following vignette describes how things went quite wrong for a young man, John, when his parents decided not to tell him that his grandfather had died:

John went to live in a group home soon after leaving school, and his parents moved to a new area some distance away. They spoke to him on the phone at least once a week, and he visited them every couple of months. A couple of years later, John became morose and uncooperative, and the staff reported that he had begun wandering off on his own and, rather worryingly, on one occasion had been missing for several hours. When he was found, he was walking in a large wood some distance from his new home.

His parents consulted a psychiatrist, who uncovered a secret. When his grandfather had died about a year earlier, his parents had decided not to take him to the funeral, even though John had had a close relationship with his grandfather. After the funeral it was hard to know how or when to tell him, and the telling was put off. His parents believed he still did not know that his grandfather had died. To make matters worse, the family dog had had to be put down, and they had not told John about this either. The significance of this became clearer when John, who seemed to have very little spoken language, drew a picture. The psychiatrist had asked him to draw a

picture of his family, but you can see that the squiggles, which might have represented family members, also spelt R.I.P. (Rest In Peace).

John's so-called "absconding" or running away was now understood as searching behaviour, and his parents were encouraged to tell him about both deaths with the help of photos and by revisiting old haunts that would remind him of his grandfather and of his dog. In the end, John responded well to several counselling sessions with a local bereavement counsellor and settled well into a new group home.

John's parents could have prepared him for the inevitability of death by beginning with the little losses occurring throughout his childhood. The "secrets" we have been mentioning could all be revealed sensitively and gradually as opportunities arose. We have tried throughout the book to give examples of how to make good use of everyday chances to be open and honest about some of the more difficult things in life.

The place of counselling

Counselling has a place for us as family members, as well as for our child. There are many times when we may have become stuck or be expending too much emotional energy coping with unresolved anxieties and conflicts, particularly ones associated with our child's impairments or the effect of these on our other children. Coming to terms with a diagnosis of learning disability, facing disappointment at missed milestones, or worrying about important decisions about long-term support needs are just some examples of times when a little professional help can move us forward again. Help should be readily available from primary-care counsellors, child and family mental health services, family therapy clinics, or learning disability specialist teams. Sometimes a life event that seems to have nothing to do with our child's disability destabilizes our adjustment. For example, bereavement may precipitate a grief reaction, which puts us in touch again with the grief we felt originally when our child's disability was first discovered.

What about counselling for our children? We have suggested that psychological help may be useful for them too, and there is growing evidence that talking therapies can be used with people with all levels of learning disability. For example, grieving people with learning disabilities are able to draw considerable benefit from bereavement counselling. Other case reports point to improvements in mental health following psychotherapy, and there is growing evidence of the effectiveness of cognitive behavioural treatments for people with mild learning disabilities. There is more interest in developing such services; however, because of the very limited provision, parents may need to be quite persistent to obtain an appropriate referral.

The Foundation for People with Learning Disabilities held a year-long enquiry in 2002 into the mental health of young people with learning disabilities and published a report, *Count Us In*, that has many useful ideas for parents and others. One of the recommendations is that preparing for adulthood needs to start well before school-leaving age. Another is that around an individual there must be information and support networks, including parents, siblings, grandparents, aunts and uncles, neighbours, family friends, a personal advisor from Connexions, a favourite college tutor, or whomever the individual wants to be involved.

8

facing the future

The book has, in the main, been organized chronologically for ease of reference, with the exception of chapter 7 where we tried to give an overview of a developmental approach to understanding personality and mental health. We thought it would be helpful to review what the parents who have spoken about their children say they have learnt about themselves and their children. Five of the children are now adults and enjoy varying degrees of independence: Carol and Patrick need twenty-four-hour care; Kirsty still lives with her parents; Jay lives in a staffed group home; and Neil shares his home with a friend, albeit with a large number of hours of dedicated support. David is still at school.

Most people find parenthood both challenging and satisfying, and we suggest that it is not really so different for parents of young people with learning disabilities. Many of "our" parents seemed somewhat surprised, looking back, to see how much turned out to be not only manageable, but also rather enjoyable and fulfilling. However, Patrick's parents disagreed:

> In the end it only became manageable by changing our own lives completely . . . we learnt that we can't be happy unless Patrick is happy and safe. Things are better for all of us now, although at huge cost in every sense.

What will have been different for all of them is that they could not rely on their preconceived ideas and expectations, but have had to take each day as it came. All will have had to do a great deal of problem solving and to develop excellent advocacy skills. If they gave up a job opportunity to support their child, they should now be able to rewrite their CVs with a long list of competencies that they didn't have twenty years previously! In fact, each of the parents of our six children have used the skills they have developed more widely, working with other parents, either in their work or in self-help groups.

They reflected on the tasks or aspects of parenting that they found easier or more difficult. For example, they said it had become quite natural to focus positively on all the attributes of their son or daughter, whether it be Carol's capacity to bring out the caring side of otherwise awkward, inconsiderate teenagers; Patrick's musicality; Jay's curiosity; Neil's sense of humour; or Kirsty's charm and excellent communication.

> Someone once referred to Carol as "an angel on Earth", by which they meant the way she brings out the best in people. For all the difficulties we have had, I can say I have never had any negative feelings towards her. With her huge eyes in her small, pretty face, and her placid, long-suffering presence, you just have to respond positively to her.

There have been many people who have worked with her, who have shown such patience. For example, her visual-impairment teacher who visited her school now teaches her at home. She works with music but has such a wonderful holistic approach to communication with Carol; I really feel she gets through to her.

But sometimes, in order to procure the benefits and the services a child needs, parents will have to focus instead on the things the child cannot do. This can be most depressing and make parents feel in some way disloyal to their child. But it is part of being a strong advocate: to be able to stand back and define what supports the person needs to live safely and well. These parents were also honest about times when they found it very hard to cope with their own feelings of grief.

We have been writing this book during a most exciting period of policy making for people with learning disabilities in the UK. It is an optimistic time in which there is promise of more independence (with increasing opportunities for supported living and supported employment); of more choice; of rights that are respected; and of laws intended to end discrimination and promote social inclusion. The aspirations of parents and young people growing up today will develop in the light of this new policy framework. One growing aspiration is for more young people to be able to have a real job. Kirsty has a paid job in an office, and Gary Butler's story told in *A New Kind of Trainer* can inspire parents and young people alike (see chapter 6).

However, another frequent reflection made by these parents was how their aspirations changed as the extent of their child's disability became apparent. No longer was there a wish for them to go to the same school as dad or mum, nor to follow in their parent's footsteps in occupational terms. For some, there was still an expectation that there would be a continuing care role and a financial commitment. It was hard to accept that their child would not be economically independent but would need to rely on state benefits. When accepted, this was also a source of some comfort as it relieved family financial responsibility. There was continuing concern about the adequacy of local authority help, and its timeliness to meet the needs of such complex children in the longer term, as well as concern about the responsibility that siblings would inevitably feel as parents became older or were no longer available to care.

> My children do feel a great responsibility towards David. I have tried to tell them that they don't need to worry. However difficult it has been for us to accept and bring up a disabled child, it will only have been for part of our lives—for them, it will be for the whole of their lives that they will have to adjust and cope.

What seemed to be more important to parents is their child's emotional stability, and their acceptance and inclusion in mainstream society, rather than their particular skills and achievements. At quite a basic level, there was the hope that their young person had in fact acquired enough skills for daily living.

We decided to give the last word to Carol and David's mother:

> Anyway, what I wanted to say was that there is light at the end of the tunnel: do not despair. The difficult phases seem to last for years, but eventually they pass. Maybe you go on to a new phase, perhaps equally or even more challenging, but there is hope!

resources

Useful contacts

Association for Supported Employment:
- www.afse.org.uk

Books Beyond Words series (picture-books for non-readers):
- www.rcpsych.ac.uk/publications/bbw

Circles Network:
- www.circlesnetwork.org.uk

Contact a Family:
- www.cafamily.org.uk

Crossroads Care (caring for carers):
- www.crossroadscare.co.uk

Down's Syndrome Association:
- www.downs-syndrome.org.uk

Every Child Matters programme:
- www.everychildmatters.gov.uk

Housing Options:
- www.housingoptions.org.uk

Information for All (advice on how to communicate simply):
- www.easyinfo.org.uk

Learning about Intellectual Disabilities and Health:
- www.intellectualdisability.info

Mencap:
- www.mencap.org.uk

Mencap Learning Disability Helpline:
- 0808 808 1111

People First (advocacy by people with learning disabilities):
- www.peoplefirst.org.uk

Sense (for people with sensory impairments):
- www.sense.org.uk

Suggested background reading

Bowlby, J. *A Secure Base: Parent–Child Attachment and Healthy Human Development.* New York: Basic Books, 1988.

Brafman, A. H. *Can You Help Me? A Guide for Parents.* London: Karnac, 2004.

Brafman, A. H. *Untying the Knot.* London: Karnac, 2001.

Carr, J. *Helping Your Handicapped Child* (2nd edition). London: Penguin, 1995.

Cichetti, D., & Beeghly, M. *Down Syndrome: A Developmental Perspective.* Cambridge: Cambridge University Press, 1990.

DeHart, G. B., Sroufe, L. A., & Cooper, R. G. *Child Development: Its Nature and Course* (4th edition). New York: McGraw-Hill, Higher Education Division, 2000.

Department of Health. *Valuing People: A New Strategy for Learning Disability in the 21st Century.* London: The Stationery Office, 2001.

Erikson, E. H. *Childhood and Society.* Harmondsworth, Middlesex: Penguin, 1965.

FPLD Enquiry. *Count Us In: The Report of the Inquiry into the Mental Health Needs of Young People with Learning Disabilities.* London: The Foundation for People with Learning Disabilities, 2002.

Fraiberg, S. *The Magic Years* (Fireside edition). New York: Simon & Schuster, 1996.

Hollins, S., & Grimer, M. *Going Somewhere: People with Mental Handicaps and Their Pastoral Care.* London: SPCK, 1988.

Owen, K., Butler, G., & Hollins, S. *A New Kind of Trainer.* London: Gaskell, 2004.

Sinason, V. *Mental Handicap and the Human Condition: New Approaches from the Tavistock.* London: Free Association Books, 1982.

Sinason, V. *Understanding Your Handicapped Child.* London: Rosendale Press, 1993.

Williams, D. *Nobody Nowhere: The Remarkable Autobiography of An Autistic Girl.* London: Jessica Kingsley, 1998.

Wing, L., & Gould, J. Severe impairments of social interaction and associated abnormalities in children: Epidemiology and classification. *Journal of Autism and Developmental Disorders, 9* (1979): 11–29.

Books Beyond Words

Books Beyond Words are A5 full-colour picture books (with supporting text at the back of each book), for people with learning or communication difficulties, their carers, and medical and other professionals. The books are developed to enable discussion about difficult life events such as bereavement, sexual abuse, visiting the doctor, going to hospital, and appearing in court. People with learning disabilities work closely with the authors throughout the development of all the books. Nine titles have been translated into Chinese.

Books Beyond Words are published jointly by St George's, University of London, and the Royal College of Psychiatrists, under the latter's Gaskell imprint.

How to Look After Your Heart, by S. Hollins, P. Adeline, & F. Cappuccio, 2005.

Looking After My Balls, by S. Hollins & J. Wilson, 2004.

When Dad Died (3rd edition), by S. Hollins & L. Sireling, 2004.

When Mum Died (3rd edition), by S. Hollins & L. Sireling, 2004.

Food . . . Fun, Healthy and Safe, by S. Hollins & M. Flynn, 2003.

When Somebody Dies, by S. Hollins, N. Blackman, & S. Dowling, 2003.

Getting on with Cancer, by V. Donaghy, J, Bernal, I. Tuffrey-Wijne, & S. Hollins, 2002.

Mugged, by S. Hollins, C. Horrocks, & V. Sinason, 2002.

Speaking Up For Myself, by S. Hollins, J. Downer, L. Farquarson, & O. Raji, 2002.

George Gets Smart, by S. Hollins, M. Flynn, & P. Russell, 2001.

Susan's Growing Up, by S. Hollins & V. Sinason, 2001.

Keeping Healthy "Down Below", by S. Hollins & J. Downer, 2000.

Looking After My Breasts, by S. Hollins & W. Perez, 2000.

Falling in Love, by S. Hollins, W. Perez, & A. Abdelnoor, 1999.

Getting On With Epilepsy, by S. Hollins, J. Bernal, & A. Thacker, 1999.

Going into Hospital, by S. Hollins, A. Avis, & S. Cheverton, 1998.

Going to Out-Patients, by S. Hollins, J. Bernal, & M. Gregory, 1998.

I Can Get Through It, by S. Hollins, C. Horrocks, & V. Sinason, 1998.

Michelle Finds a Voice, by S. Hollins & S. Barnett, 1997.

Going to the Doctor, by S. Hollins, J. Bernal, & M. Gregory, 1996.

You're On Trial, by S. Hollins, I. Clare, & G. Murphy, 1996.

You're Under Arrest, by S. Hollins, I. Clare, & G. Murphy, 1996.

Feeling Blue, by S. Hollins & J. Curran, 1995.

Making Friends, by S. Hollins & T. Roth, 1995.

Going to Court, by S. Hollins, V. Sinason, & J. Boniface, 1994.

Hug Me Touch Me, by S. Hollins & T. Roth, 1994.

A New Home in the Community, by S. Hollins & D. Hutchinson, 1993.

Bob Tells All, by S. Hollins & V. Sinason, 1993.

Peter's New Home, by S. Hollins & D. Hutchinson, 1993.

Jenny Speaks Out, by S. Hollins & V. Sinason, 1992.

pen portraits

Six children with learning disabilities

These short descriptions of the six children whose stories illustrate the book are repeated here for ease of reference.

Three of the children were diagnosed as having a learning disability at birth:

- — "Kirsty", who is now an adult, and "David", who is still at school, both have Down's syndrome.
- — "Carol", who was not expected to survive to adulthood, is a 20-year-old with profound and multiple learning disabilities and with very high support needs.

"Patrick", "Neil", and "Jay", now all young adults, differ in the time of their diagnosis, the degree of their learning disability, and the extent of their behavioural challenges to their carers:

- — Patrick is autistic and has a severe learning disability and challenging behaviour.
- — Neil has a moderate learning disability, with specific language difficulties.
- — Jay also has a moderate learning disability, with a specific medical syndrome.

Kirsty

Kirsty is the youngest of five children in a family who live in the suburbs of a large city. Her diagnosis of Down's syndrome was a considerable shock to her parents, who had no previous knowledge of anyone with a learning disability. Her mother, especially, as she learnt more about Kirsty's condition, became very involved with other families who had a disabled child. She found that other families valued her interest and support and that this was of mutual benefit. Kirsty had a heart murmur and had regular checks by a paediatric cardiologist until she was 16 years old. She also had a hearing problem and had grommets fitted when she was 7 years old, but generally she has enjoyed good health throughout her life. Having older brothers and sisters meant she had a ready social circle. She attended the local special school for delicate children and did well until she was a teenager.

During a brief period at a school for children with severe learning disabilities, her academic achievement deteriorated. Her education continued in a special class in the local adult education college, and she still attends a part-time basic skills course in maths. Kirsty is now 25 and is a very able young woman, both academically and artistically.

David

David, who is Carol's younger brother and the third child in his family of four siblings, has Down's syndrome. He had initial health problems (co-anal atresia, a bony blockage in the nasal passage), with difficulty in breathing. He had an emergency operation at the age of 2 weeks and on-going treatment for a year. He also suffered from glue ear and hearing problems and had several sets of grommets and "T" tubes, and hearing aids were tried. He also suffered from a constant runny nose and frequent infections. He attended a mainstream primary school and now goes to a local special school. It is hoped he will go on to a local further education college. He enjoys a full social life, including a special needs drama group, youth club, and sports club. He likes going out to football matches, swimming, watching videos, and eating out in cafes! He is a well-built, healthy 17-year-old, showing improved communication skills and sociability.

Carol

Carol is the second in a family with four children. She was born with severe brain damage caused by cytomegalovirus. She had frequent seizures as a tiny baby, and these have continued throughout her life. Gradually it became apparent that she had serious visual and hearing impairments, and cerebral palsy (spastic quadriplegia). She attended a local special school and remains living at home, with her mother as her main carer. She now has scoliosis and curvature of the spine. Carol is now a profoundly multi-disabled young woman aged 20 years. She is passive and quite unresponsive. She is totally dependent on others for all aspects of her personal care and daily living. She often has difficulty eating and is frequently sick. She receives some limited extra help from paid carers and enjoys a sensory programme of activities such as physiotherapy, aromatherapy, swimming, music, and light therapy. She attends a hospice for respite care.

Patrick

Patrick has an older brother and sister and has enjoyed being in the centre of a close family. He was a beautiful baby, and the reality of his delayed development unfolded gradually. He is now known to be autistic, but this was still a little-understood condition when he was a young child and the detailed diagnosis came much later. He also developed epilepsy in his teenage years. Patrick eventually gained a fairly good use of language (although like many autistic people he took a long time to sort out his use of I/you and mine/your). He failed to cope in three special schools before he was 10 years old, and then he went to live in a special community school with the hope that he would move on to a residential adult college and residential care. He has always needed people around him who really understand his view of the world and his fears. In the absence of understanding, his behaviour can become unmanageable, so he has experienced many crises of environment and support. His mother eventually gave up work entirely to be available sometimes as his full-time carer, sometimes as an advocate, and latterly as his care manager. He now lives in his own home with a team of carers who enable him to continue to enjoy the full life his family gave him as he was growing up.

Neil

Neil was born to parents who already had a 2-year-old daughter. Neil now has two younger sisters as well. He was an easy baby, with no indication of a disability until he was about 18 months old, when a hearing problem was suspected and thought to be contributing to his delayed development. Over the next few years Neil had numerous assessments, by doctors, psychologists, and educators, with no clear diagnosis. He had meanwhile attended playschool and a mainstream nursery but still had no useful speech or comprehension. The choice of primary school was made on the basis of the speech therapy available there. The school included many autistic children, though Neil's needs seemed different from many of his classmates. His parents chose a boarding-school for him when he was 11 years old, after visiting many other schools. Its warm, relaxed approach and the way teachers and speech therapists worked together proved successful. Neil stayed on until 18, developing considerable social competence with language.

After leaving school he chose to attend a residential college, distant from home. This was not successful, so he moved to a group home in London, where he enjoyed a close social network both in his house group and in the wider community. He spent most of his weekdays in craft workshops. After a while he decided he wanted to live more independently. He moved into his own flat, sharing with a friend and with the substantial support they both needed.

Jay

Jay is the only child of Indian parents who had come to England a few years before his birth to continue their studies. He is now 24 years old.

Jay has a rare syndrome, with several aspects to it, including learning disability, congenital heart disease, and epilepsy. He also has to face the stigma of looking different—just as Kirsty and David have to.

Jay was assessed by an educational psychologist before starting school and was offered a place in a special school for children with severe learning disabilities. His parents had heard that it was possible for children like Jay to have extra help in order to support them in a mainstream school. A local church primary school accepted Jay on trial for a term, provided that one of his parents accompanied him for at least part of each day. His father worked part time during this period so that he could take on this role, and Jay remained in mainstream education until it was time to transfer to secondary school. Then it was decided that the comprehensive school would be too intimidating an environment for Jay. When he was 18 years old, he developed epilepsy. The watchful eye needed to help him cope with epileptic seizures was more reliable in a special school. After school he had two years in a residential college and then moved to a staffed group home near his parents, where he currently lives. He attends a day centre for adults with learning disabilities.

index